THE CONSERVATIVE OPPORTUNITY

THE CONSERVATIVE OPPORTUNITY

edited by

Lord Blake and John Patten

with a Foreword by

Lord Hailsham of St Marylebone

M

First published 1976 by
THE MACMILLAN PRESS LTD
London and Basingstoke
Associated companies in New York
Dublin Melbourne Johannesburg and Madras

SBN 333 19971 5 (hardcover)
SBN 333 19972 3 (paperback)

Typeset by
PREFACE LTD
Salisbury, Wilts
and printed in Great Britain by
BILLING & SONS LTD
Guildford, Worcester and London

Contents

Foreword

It is now more than a quarter of a century since I wrote *The Case for Conservatism*. It was written in the immediate aftermath of the defeat of 1945, at a time when it was common talk in the press that the Conservative Party would never again rise to power for at least a generation. In fact the process of recovery took six years; and from 1951 to 1964 and again from 1970 to 1974 the Conservative Party was the leading influence in the state.

The scene has shifted since 1946, and, though I would not wish myself to unsay anything I wrote down as fundamental to Conservatism thirty years ago, circumstances have again arisen which make it necessary for Conservatives to write and think afresh about their fundamental role in Britain. It is right that the task should be undertaken by a group of younger writers, and I am delighted that Lord Blake is the joint editor and author of the opening chapter.

Since 1946 the new factors which have entered into the situation seem to me to be as follows. When *The Case for Conservatism* was written I was basically advocating a return to the old philosophy of the two-party system in which each of the two parties respected the contribution of the other, and each allowed its opponent to make that characteristic contribution from time to time.

We are now faced with what has come to be called the 'ratchet effect' of Socialism. Our main opponent is deeply committed to make irreversible changes in our society which progressively leave less and less room for the kind of values in which Conservatives believe. How must Conservatives react to this sinister development without creating a polarity between the parties inconsistent with parliamentary government?

Then we were concerned to provide a safety net of social security adequate to prevent a recurrence of pre-war unemployment and poverty. Today we are concerned to secure adequate rewards and investment to make any kind of plural society possible. The enemy then was insecurity. The enemy today is uniformity, which has grown to the extent of becoming altogether incompatible with freedom.

Today it is possible to show that, in any part of the world where it has been tried, Socialism has failed to provide an adequate range of goods, services, or agricultural products. At the same time we are faced with a constitutional crisis largely brought on by the process of over-centralisation, over-government, and excessive taxation. This constitutional crisis is largely produced by Socialist collectivism.

Lurking behind the constitutional crisis is the growing insecurity of the international scene. For a long time consensus politics have been possible in foreign policy, despite party differences. How long will this continue to be possible in the present state of left-wing opinion?

Industrial relations have once more become a party issue. Are good relations with militant forces in the trade union movement compatible with our duty to the nation, and the minimum economic policy to secure survival?

Thirty years ago the problem of education was simply to provide enough teachers and schools to man the secondary system introduced by the Butler Act. Today the problem is whether the Socialist mania for social engineering and comprehensivisation is compatible at all with proper educational standards and a reasonable measure of parental choice.

So this book is timely. I wish it all success.

HAILSHAM

March 1976

Acknowledgements

We are very happy to acknowledge the help and encouragement that we received from the Baroness Young, Christopher Patten (Director of the Conservative Research Department) and Professor Max Beloff (Principal of University College at Buckingham) in the early stages of planning this book. The original idea of producing such a volume by people teaching in or closely connected with the University of Oxford grew out of a meeting of the Oxford Region of the National Association of Conservative Graduates in the winter of 1974. Miss Sarah King-Turner expertly typed the final manuscript.

BLAKE

The Queen's College, Oxford

JOHN PATTEN

Hertford College, Oxford

March 1976

Notes on the Contributors

ERIC BARENDT is a Fellow of St Catherine's College, Oxford. He was previously on the staff of the Law Commission. His special interests are constitutional and administrative law, and he is writing a book on the law of social security.

LORD BLAKE (Robert Blake), created a life peer in 1971, is Provost of The Queen's College, Oxford, and has been a member of the City Council. His publications include *The Private Papers of Douglas Haig*, *The Unknown Prime Minister*, *Disraeli*, *The Conservative Party from Peel to Churchill* and *The Office of Prime Minister*.

VERNON BOGDANOR is Fellow and Tutor in Politics at Brasenose College, Oxford. He is a member of Oxfordshire County Council and vice-chairman of its Education Committee. In addition to contributions to journals he has edited *The Age of Affluence, 1951–1964* and *Disraeli's Lothair*.

LORD GOWRIE, who was at Balliol, was a junior Minister in the Heath Government (1970–4) and a spokesman on industrial relations in the House of Lords. He has been a tutor at Harvard and a lecturer at University College, London.

JOHN PATTEN is a Fellow of Hertford College, Oxford. He has been a member of the City Council and is prospective Conservative Parliamentary candidate for the city.

GILLIAN PEELE is Fellow and Tutor in Politics at Lady Margaret Hall, Oxford. Her publications include *The Politics of Reappraisal, 1918–1939* (with Chris Cook) and *The Government of the United Kingdom* (with Max Beloff, forthcoming). She is on the editorial board of *Crossbow*.

JOHN REDWOOD is a Fellow of All Souls College and now a merchant banker, having been a tutor in economic history at Oxford. He is a member of the Oxfordshire County Council and a governor of Oxford Polytechnic.

GRAHAM RICHARDS is Fellow and Tutor in Chemistry at Brasenose College, Oxford. He is the author of more than a hundred scientific papers and of four books. He has been Visiting Professor at the University of California, Berkeley, and Visiting Scholar at Stanford University.

PETER SINCLAIR is Fellow and Tutor in Economics at Brasenose College, Oxford. He is on the editorial board of *Oxford Economic Papers* and is writing a book on macroeconomics and monetary theory.

ANN SPOKES, who was at St Anne's College, Oxford, is a local administrator at Oxford for Age Concern and a member of the District and County Councils. She has been a Conservative candidate in three Parliamentary elections, and Lord Mayor of the City of Oxford.

The Hon. C. M. WOODHOUSE has been Director of the Royal Institute of International Affairs, a Visiting Fellow of Nuffield College, Oxford, and MP for Oxford. His publications include *British Foreign Policy since the Second World War*.

1 A Changed Climate

LORD BLAKE

The Conservative Party is going through a period of major rethinking for the first time since 1945—50. These essays are intended as a contribution towards that process. Nearly all of them concern home affairs and these must be our major preoccupation just now, but I also commend Monty Woodhouse's unorthodox essay on foreign policy and Graham Richards's brief but highly stimulating piece on Conservatism and Science.

Political parties seldom philosophise when in office. Their leaders are too preoccupied by administrative pressures, too concerned with immediate problems to have the leisure to reflect on the broad purposes for which their party exists. Ministers may not in theory believe that a week in politics is a long time, but they tend to behave as if they believed it. The experience of defeat, however, concentrates the political mind wonderfully, and people who have never given serious thought to such matters begin to reflect on what has gone wrong and to puzzle how to put it right. Conservatives of many types and attitudes have been doing this since the loss of the two elections in 1974.

Curiously enough, there was no similar process after the party's second major setback in the post-war era, the loss of the 1966 election. It is not easy to say quite why; it may be that the shock was not enough; unlike 1945 and 1974 the upshot was expected long before, and perhaps a certain degree of consternation is needed to galvanise a party. Moreover, the obvious difficulties into which Mr Wilson ran so soon after his victory, together with the indications of by-election results and the opinion polls, made an intellectual reformulation of fundamental beliefs seem unnecessary. It looked as if the Conservatives would win, whatever their 'philosophy' was. When in early 1970 the same indicators suddenly began to show a swing back to Labour, it was far too late for thought. Nor, as matters turned out, was it needed. Contrary to almost every prediction, the Conservatives won easily. Historians will long debate the reasons. It is to be hoped that they will not underestimate the courage, tenacity and sheer will to win of Mr Heath, who never wavered in spite of the darkness and gloom. But his determination could not have been the only cause; the reasons why people vote as they do remain mysterious.

Whatever the explanation of their victory, the Conservatives did not win because the intellectual tide was flowing in their favour. That is not to say that between 1966 and 1970 they lacked policies on particular issues — and policies sharply different from Labour's. Mr Heath was no 'Butskellite', witness the play made by Mr Wilson over 'Selsdon Man', parodied as a symbol of flinty reaction — electioneering rodomontade, of course, but a sign that Mr Heath's was not the Conservatism of the soft centre. The party has seldom in modern times adumbrated a larger number of specific policies — arguably *too* many and *too* specific. Back in the mid-nineteenth century Lord Derby writing to Disraeli said that he 'always . . . deprecated the practice . . . of starting detailed projects in opposition'. It might have been wiser if the manifesto had been less categorical in some matters, incomes policy for example.

The Conservatives did not go into the election of 1970 devoid of policies, but they did go into it without the sort of freshly articulated doctrinal support which they had enjoyed twenty years earlier from such diverse thinkers as Hayek and Lord Hailsham. The outlook of comment-ators, economists, intellectuals, journalists — the opinion-formers in general — was anti-Conservative. The accepted 'philosophy' was still *dirigiste*. Planning, high public expenditure, high taxation, a rising role for the State remained the accepted shibboleths, however doubtful some people may have become about their practical manifestations during the chaotic last years of Harold Wilson's first administration. There was no serious challenge in intellectual circles to this orthodoxy. The Con-servatives did not win the election because they had won 'the battle for the mind', rather because of a general discontent about high prices and sheer governmental incompetence.

This somewhat ambivalent position was reflected in the new administration's record; the Cabinet began with the intention of 'getting government off the people's backs', but, lacking any clear intellectual mandate to do so, somehow ended with an even larger number of public employees in the non-productive sector than ever before. It began with a determination to abandon lame ducks and avoid all forms of intervention in wage-fixing, but it ended by capitulating to the sit-in at Upper Clyde Shipbuilders and by trying to impose the most complete statutory wage policy ever attempted. No doubt there were cogent reasons for all these and other U-turns. It is also fair to say that the Heath Government was dogged by much bad luck. No one could easily have foreseen the quadrupling of oil prices which followed the Arab oil embargo, and which effectively wrecked the Government's economic policy of expansion in order to break out of 'stop-go'. Nevertheless, it is hard to believe that an administration which felt that it had a firm doctrinal base, and an intellectually legitimate ideology (by which I mean one that was accepted by a substantial section of the opinion-formers), would have diverged quite so far from the principles which it had been proclaiming before it came back into power.

Another symptom of this disorientation was the apparent lack of a guiding purpose in its policies. The Conservatives in 1970 had given the impression that they were opposed to any enhancement of the 'welfare consensus' (i.e. to the augmentation of the 'social wage' at the expense of take-home pay). They also gave the impression that they would lower national and local government expenditure, reduce taxes, and in general adopt a policy of minimum governmental interference. These were attitudes on which the elements in the Party distinguished by Andrew Gamble in his interesting book, *The Conservative Nation* (1974), as the 'Right Progressives' and the 'New Right' could agree. The New Right might go further and wish to reduce the ratio of public expenditure to gross domestic product by more than the Right Progressives would like. But no Conservative of any complexion could have set out with the object of actually increasing it. Yet this was what happened.

Taxes were cut, it is true – but not by very much, and mainly by adding to budget deficits. Public employment rose almost as fast under the Conservatives as it had under Labour. The National Health Service was reorganised in a manner which so far appears to have increased the number of officials and the remoteness of the service without bringing any obvious medical benefits. The Local Government Act was an even more unfortunate measure. Its author says that no one had a bad word for it at the time. It would be nice if anyone had a good word for it now. The passage of the Act has been followed by the proliferation of an overpaid and very unpopular bureaucracy. In the field of devolution its implications, as Eric Barendt says in his essay, are particularly inconvenient. Scotland, under the proposals of the latest White Paper [November 1975], could have no less than six tiers of government. The Conservatives are not responsible for the latest White Paper, but was devolution unpredictable in 1972?

The Heath Cabinet had not got much of a record to present to its supporters in 1974. It had brought Britain into the EEC, but this, however valuable as an achievement, was not a popular cause at the time. Its legislation in the matter of health, pensions, local government, water and housing, could be variously assessed, but nothing was there to inspire the imagination. The Government's taxation reforms were claimed to be as drastic as any in the past century. One may set aside the question whether a greater degree of efficiency in collecting taxes is a particularly heart-warming 'cry' for the Conservative Party at an election. What most Conservatives want is lower taxation. This they had indeed been given since 1970, but inflation was rapidly eroding its effective benefit. People did not feel as if the burden had been lifted at all substantially.

The final result of the election no doubt turned far less on the Conservative legislative record than on the particular circumstances in which a snap dissolution was called. The general point remains that the Conservatives embarked in 1970 on a new course which did not *at that time* – and this is a point of key importance – appear intellectually reputable. Lacking complete conviction in their own policies, constantly

criticised by the 'opinion-formers', who still favoured a sort of Lab/Lib/
Whitehall consensus, ministers under what they believed to be the pressure
of circumstances made a *volte-face*. One can only marvel that the
February election of 1974 actually gave them a higher share of the popular
vote than Labour and that in October they held as much ground as they
did.

If the intellectual atmosphere is going to be the same at the next general
election, whenever that may be, there would be little prospect of
Conservative success, except in the event of a major economic crisis, some
traumatic débâcle such as split the Labour Party in 1931. In fact, however,
there are signs of one of those rare and profound changes in the
intellectual climate which occur only once or twice in a hundred years,
like the triumph of the entrepreneurial ethos in nineteenth-century
England, or the rise of Voltairean scepticism in eighteenth-century France,
or the disappearance of Puritanism after 1660. There is a wind of change
in Britain and much of the democratic world – and it comes from the
right, not the left.

In New Zealand and Australia parties very similar to the British Labour
Party were blown out of office at the end of 1975, although in both
countries they seemed to command solid trade union support. In Australia
this occurred despite a constitutional crisis of the first magnitude, which
might easily have had damaging repercussions on the Opposition parties. In
Germany there are many signs that the CDU-CSU may win the election
due this year, and even if it does not, that the SDP will have to move
markedly to the right in order to hold on. In the United States, who would
have given a fig for the Republicans' chances after Mr Nixon's resignation?
It still seems scarcely possible that they could win, but their chances are
being taken far more seriously than they were two years ago.

Within Britain the signs of an intellectual revolt against the orthodoxies
which have ruled public life since the early 1940s are becoming more and
more obvious. The great high priest of deficit finance and of spending or
borrowing our way out of depression is losing his posthumous ascendancy.
Keynes is no longer a name to conjure with. Or perhaps (since Keynes was
much more cautious than many of his disciples – see his famous exposure
of the ills of inflation) we should say that the Keynesian image is no longer
being worshipped. The secret of Keynes seemed to be that a country by
deficit finance and high public expenditure could achieve full employment, an expanding economy and a stable currency. This apparently
worked for nearly a quarter of a century, but the pursuit of these policies
in latter years appears to have produced a stagnant economy, the highest
unemployment since the nineteen-thirties and the worst inflation since the
sixteenth century.

These intellectual and practical doubts about the hitherto accepted
economic consensus are reinforced by misgivings about the welfare

consensus. Taxation has now reached such colossal proportions that even Labour ministers are beginning to be uneasy about it. Twenty years ago a married man with three children reached the standard rate of income tax only if his income was nearly double (actually 1.9 times) national average earnings. Today he reaches it if his income is two-fifths of the national average. This means that when a silly, improvident and blackmailable government pours in £162 million to 'rescue' jobs in Chrysler, it is in effect asking a large number of wage-earners well below the national average to contribute heavily to the preservation of jobs for a large number who earn two or three times as much. This lunacy cannot continue for long after it has been understood — and it soon will be understood if the Conservative Party does its job properly.

It is one thing for the average earner to be in favour of a high social wage when it is 'free', i.e. when it comes from what would otherwise have been the take-home pay of the bourgeoisie and is thus a straight addition to his effective income. It is quite another matter when the average earner largely pays for it himself. He is bound sooner or later to ask the questions put thus by Mr David Howell, Conservative MP for Guildford, in *The Times* (9 January 1976):

> Are the public services we now pay for properly tailored to our local needs, as against bureaucratic Whitehall or County Hall views about what our needs are supposed to be? If we kept the money and spent it ourselves, rather than having it recycled through a slow and bureaucratic apparatus, might we get a better bargain?

These are questions which go to the heart of the matter. They raise a major query about the 'welfare consensus'. The hallmark of 'progress' has been seen by an entire generation of liberal/left middle-class intellectuals in terms of rising expenditure on social services. The amount of the 'social wage' (measured, incidentally, by very dubious calculations) has been one of the bull points in Socialist propaganda. But if both Keynesian doctrine of high public expenditure for economic management, and the welfare consensus doctrine of the high social wage face intellectual fire and mass discontent, then we are indeed moving into a very different climate of opinion.

These criticisms of the accepted orthodoxies have been enhanced by — and closely connected with — a surge of feeling against 'bureaucracy' which suddenly swelled up in late 1975 and early 1976. The high inflation-proof pensions of top-level civil servants, the suspicion that Whitehall and County Hall 'advice' usually leads to ever more public employees at rates of pay which outstrip those of industry, the very big awards made as a result of arbitration by Lords Boyle and Houghton, all contributed to this sense of runaway bureaucratic extravagance.

Some of these attacks in the press and elsewhere have been unfair and over-personified. It is certainly true that the public sector has expanded to a dangerous degree at the expense of the private sector of labour available for 'marketable products' [see Bacon and Eltis, *Britain's Economic Problem* (1976)]. It is also true that bureaucracy has a self-perpetuating and self-proliferating quality which leads, unless deliberately checked, to unlimited expansion. But the responsibility lies in the end, not with public servants, but with successive governments, Labour and Conservative. After all, they are not *obliged* to create the new institutions, organisations, committees, centres, etc., which consume such an unnecessarily vast and increasingly resented proportion of the national income, even if their officials advise them to do so — which is by no means always the case.

These are not the only signs of a move to the right in the Western world. Terrorism has made a great many people whose 'liberal' instinct was to be against the army and the police believe that there is something to be said for 'law and order'. Increased expenditure on that part of the public sector would be widely acclaimed and, if the cost has to be recovered, as it must be, by economies in other parts, this is now far more acceptable than it would have been ten or even five years ago. Who would weep if the bureaucracy set up by the Community Land Act, the Equal Opportunities Commission, and the Consumer Centres — to name only a few of the follies erected by recent legislation — were to be swept away and their funds diverted to reinforcing the security of the citizen and the nation? The money thus gained might not be a very large sum, but it would be a symbol — and symbols can matter.

There are many other signs of a swing to the right. As John Vaizey put it [*Times Educational Supplement*, 26 December 1975, p. 4], 'The trendy lefties who were the apotheosis of the 1960s and early 1970s look like dinosaurs.'

This is particularly striking in the field of education dealt with in the chapter by Vernon Bogdanor. The Black Papers which were the object of ridicule a few years ago among the educational establishment are not so easily laughed off now. If 'progressive education' means an increasing proportion of illiterates and innumerates, parents are not going to tolerate it much more. The row about the William Tyndale Junior School is a portent for the future. The Secretary of State is no longer being briefed by his civil servants in the DES to talk a lot of drivel about 'new maps of learning', but instead to make a favourable reference to discipline and the three Rs. In secondary education the performance of comprehensive schools is regarded with increasing scepticism, and the Conservatives when they get back are bound to override the Department and insist on a major inquiry. Moreover, they will have a great deal of public support if they restore the Direct Grant Regulations, and do so in a form which can only be altered by the repeal of an Act of Parliament.

Education is not the only area to feel the wind of change. The social services discussed by Ann Spokes are increasingly under fire because of the

Labour faith in what she calls 'an average standard of universal indiscriminate benefits for all'. The utter failure of housing policy cogently analysed by John Patten is an example of the contradictions and absurdities which follow from another type of doctrinaire egalitarianism. These atavistic memories of the means test and the wicked landlord are curious examples of the encrusted small 'c' conservatism of the Labour mind, and they have in the past had far more influence than they should on Conservative thought too — or at any rate on Conservative practice.

There remains the area of life where antique prejudices are more hardened, ancient beliefs more fossilised and enlightened change more difficult than anywhere else — the trade unions. The question of industrial relations is dealt with in the chapter by Lord Gowrie. Conservatives should not be too despondent about the prospects. Because the trade unions forced Mr Wilson to reverse his policy in 1969 and overthrew Mr Heath's Government in 1974, it does not necessarily follow that they will always win every such confrontation, or that they will always press every wage claim regardless of the national interest. They, too, are not insulated from a changing intellectual climate. The connection between inflation and unemployment must by now have become apparent to their more thoughtful leaders. Moderates have been doing much better at recent elections than extremists. It is possible that trade union leaders will come to see, as their counterparts in many other countries have seen long ago, that stifling taxation, a top-heavy public sector and a profitless economy are as bad for them as for everyone else. They too may wish to keep more of their pay packet for themselves and have less of it recycled through Whitehall and County Hall.

If this assessment of a changing intellectual climate is anywhere near to reality, then the Conservatives have an excellent chance of recovering power, and of doing so on the basis of a new orthodoxy replacing the old one created in the war years, a new concept of the relationship between government and people. How this might be done was broadly adumbrated by Mrs Thatcher in her splendid keynote speech to the 1975 Conservative Conference at Blackpool, when she urged the case for less government, less interference, more freedom for the ordinary person to get on with his work unhindered by bureaucracy, and more freedom for him to do what he wishes with more of his own money. Mr Heath said just the same in his day. The difference is that the climate of opinion has changed. What could plausibly, though wrongly, be dismissed in 1970 as 'reactionary' amidst giggles from Hampstead cannot be laughed off today.

These essays attempt to examine some, by no means all, of the areas of policy which a future Conservative Cabinet might wish to consider. There are suggestions with which many Conservatives would not agree. Eric Barendt in his chapter on constitutional reform argues for proportional representation and a Bill of Rights. In 1975 change in our electoral system was rejected by the Party Conference at Blackpool in emphatic terms, but the arguments against a mode of election which makes it possible for a party supported by 39 per cent of the popular vote to have a majority of seats and, moreover, to be dominated by a minority within that 39 per cent, deserve careful consideration; bombast is not enough. The implacable hatred of the Labour Party for electoral reform is in itself a reason for Conservatives to think again.

There is, however, one electoral reform which is not mentioned by Mr Barendt, but which even the most traditionalist Tory might well look at favourably. What possible justification is there today for allowing the million citizens of the Irish Republic resident in Britain to exercise the vote? No other country in the world confers the franchise on aliens. Irish citizens have been aliens ever since Eire left the Commonwealth and became an independent foreign country. It has been reckoned that the 'Irish vote', in that sense of the words, divided 84 per cent Labour and 16 per cent Conservative in the 1970 general election [see Butler and Pinto-Duschinsky, *The British General Election of 1970*, p. 408]. It would seem common sense for the next Conservative Government to disfranchise a category of people who have no moral claim whatever to vote in British general elections.

A Bill of Rights is on the face of it a more attractive constitutional reform to Conservatives than proportional representation, but it too raises difficulties. Eric Barendt points out that the entrenchment of certain freedoms could be interpreted in a way which would not enthuse Conservatives, who are on the whole against 'the permissive society' — and with good reason. That, they might say, can be left to the good or bad offices of Mr Roy Jenkins. Nevertheless, the case for a Bill of Rights in a constitution which is virtually unicameral is a very strong one, and it could well fit in with plans for devolution.

The chapter on constitutional reform is important because along with Gillian Peele's essay on Conservative 'philosophy', it raises a central question about the sort of Conservatism for which this book argues. There have been in the past two sometimes conflicting and contradictory traditions in the party's attitude — paternalism and libertarianism. There has been a case in the past for paternalistic interventionism to soften the rigours of doctrinaire *laissez-faire* capitalism. All this belongs to the days when the Liberal Party of Cobden and Bright was the enemy. It is largely irrelevant now. The common feature of all the essays in this book which deal with home affairs is libertarianism — less government, less public expenditure, fewer public servants, lower taxation, greater freedom. The enemy is not *laissez-faire*, but *étatisme*. Paternalism is out, along with the welfare consensus.

We have reached a parting of the ways in terms of attitudes to society and economic management. In 1963, as John Redwood points out in his essay on managing the economy, public expenditure absorbed 43 per cent of the gross national product. If anyone had then predicted that in twelve years' time the figure would be 60 per cent, he would have been laughed out of court. Yet this is what has happened, and for over a third of that period the Conservatives have been in office. If the increase goes on at this rate 'the public sector will consume the whole of the gross domestic product before the end of this century'. An important wing of the Labour Party would like to see just such a development. It is, after all, the situation of an East European 'people's republic'. By rendering it virtually impossible for independent firms to thrive and by then claiming that they have 'failed the nation', the extreme left which dominated Mr Wilson's Government during 1974 and much of 1975 was bidding fair to achieve this object; and that element in the Party has by no means given up yet. The logical outcome of their policies would be a wartime siege economy, rationing, direction of labour, State planning with its in-competence and corruption − the whole country being run by a cumbrous and soulless bureaucracy which would soon stifle liberty. Ironically, the earliest freedoms to vanish would be those of speech and writing, followed closely by that of trade unions to bargain with their only employer − the State. It would be some slight consolation to the rest of us if Mr Foot and Mr Benn were the first to go the way of Mr Dubcek − but not much.

The majority of the Labour Cabinet and probably of the Parliamentary Party still believe in a 'mixed economy', but they remain instinctively averse to profits and the private sector, instinctively favourable to high public expenditure and heavy taxation. They hope that somehow round the corner the economy will pick up and that 'growth' will finance their social policies in the end, though even Mr Healey has had to concede that there must be a halt for the time being.

The truth which cannot be hammered home too strongly by the Conservative Party is that the economy will never expand sufficiently to finance social policies of the sort in which Labour believes, as long as the existing pattern of public provision continues. If we come out strongly in favour of extending the area in which market forces operate, and reducing, not merely halting, public expenditure, this stems from no desire to lower standards in health, education and social services, etc. On the contrary there is general agreement that the level of such provision in most of the other EEC countries is higher than ours. Yet their public sector is considerably smaller and their method of financing the social services is markedly different, more selective, less reliant upon taxation. Is there no lesson to be learnt from this? Labour certainly will never learn it. The Conservatives must, and the British electorate may soon come to appreciate that a greater reliance on the market will bring a greater prosperity and higher standards for everyone: 'social profitability' might be a good slogan.

There is, however, one thing that it will not bring − and the Conservatives must face the fact. That is greater 'equality'. Gillian Peele makes the case for what she describes as a society of 'principled pluralism' both on economic and social grounds. The whole concept is incompatible with the sort of equality favoured by Socialists. Peter Sinclair points out in his essay on the economic role of the State that efficiency, liberty and equality are not naturally compatible if people vary in skill and earning power (as they always do). Coercion and direction of labour may achieve equality and efficiency − of a sort, but efficiency, in a society which respects liberty, will never be achieved if there are no incentives and if the marginal tax rate on the top earned incomes remains at the ludicrous figure of 83 per cent. The Conservative record over taxation since 1951 has been far too cautious. Why should a Conservative Government not firmly set its sights at never taking more than half a man's gross income or half of his 'transferred capital'? And why not 'index' taxation bands in general? The Treasury, it is said, would be furious. The Treasury, in the words of Winston Churchill in another context, should be on tap, not on top.

The Conservative Party never has stood for 'equality'. It stands for *equality of opportunity* − a very different concept. What it also stands for − and the two concepts are closely connected − is a 'fair' society, one in which endeavour is rewarded and in which people feel that they are in the true sense getting what they deserve. The welfare consensus combined with crushing taxation has made them begin to feel that this is no longer a 'fair' society.

There is more of a desire to get government off our backs than there has been since 1950. The Conservative Party has an excellent chance of profiting from this mood. It is significant how utterly devoid of intellectual excitement, new thought or fresh ideas Labour has become. It is significant that the essays in this book are largely written by younger academics and Oxonians − a category which for an entire generation was a major source of recruitment to the left. Elections are not won by 'intellectuals' nor by those who draft policies; but intellectual attitudes do in some mysterious way affect a wider opinion.

The Conservative Party would be very ill-advised at this stage to commit itself to much in the way of detail. What is needed, rather, is an ideological frame of reference, a set of general criteria by which solutions to particular problems can be judged. If the foregoing analysis of the popular mood is at all correct, the first of these criteria is a massive reduction in public expenditure and in the public sector of employment. It is not enough to have a standstill. It is essential to reverse a trend which has had such ruinous effects on the national economy during the last few years. Conservatives should not − and the more realistic among them do not − pretend that this will be easy. There may be a general feeling that we are over-governed locally and nationally, but there is sure to be an outcry at almost every specific cut-back. A Conservative Government will have to harden its heart to these protests, and it will have to turn a deaf ear to bright young officials 'identifying new needs' and discovering fresh areas of social welfare – or at any rate pay no attention until other bright young officials have discovered a method of saving on old needs.

The instinctive Labour reaction when a callous mother starves her baby to death and the social services, through incompetence, have failed to stop the disaster, is naturally one of horror. It is quickly succeeded by the cry that, if only £150,000 more had been spent on the services of that particular local authority, the tragedy would not have happened. The instinctive Conservative reaction is also one of horror. Such an event is indeed a dreadful tragedy. But is it going to occur less often if more money is spent on the social services? Is there not such a thing as original sin? Cruel and evil people exist at all times in all forms of society. The Conservative reaction is that these people are at least in some degree less likely to commit their crimes if exemplary sentences are given to offenders, and that incompetence among social workers will at least in some degree be reduced if it results in prompt dismissal from a well-paid job instead of the usual bleat that 'we are all guilty'.

It is essential for a Conservative Government to make real cuts in actual expenditure, not just cuts in future programmes envisaging increased expenditure. The present Government's White Paper on public expenditure [Cmnd 6393] has not even begun to grasp this nettle. It is as if a man who has long known that he is heading for bankruptcy were to announce that he will put things straight by buying a diamond necklace for his wife in Christmas 1977 instead of a diamond necklace *and* a mink coat, as he had originally planned. The uproar on the left of the Labour Party and the resignation of a minor minister should not deceive the public – and certainly not the Conservative Party – into the belief that there has been any real acceptance by this very left-wing government of the need to cut the percentage of gross national product taken by public expenditure to much below its current level. In practice the most that Mr Healey is likely to achieve is stabilisation at something like the present ruinous figure of 60 per cent.

It is vital for the Conservative Party to proclaim its intention – and act accordingly in office – of shifting resources from the public to the private sector on a very substantial scale. At least £5000 million is the order of magnitude; this would involve an immense reduction of transfer payments including subsidies of every sort for food, houses and above all the nationalised industries.

These are very big changes, but they would also have a lot of support from classes in society which have by no means been accustomed to vote Conservative. There is intense and rising resentment at present income tax levels throughout the country. A great many people would accept, as Conservatives do, elimination of poverty as a social objective, but would not accept 'equality'. The two purposes are poles apart and the financial implications are entirely different; the former is much cheaper than the latter. A Conservative administration which reduced taxation, spread home ownership, allowed a real parental choice in education, and at least paved the way for a major structural change in the welfare state by substituting 'insurance' payments for health and education in the place of blanket general taxation could create one of those 'irreversible changes' which no subsequent government could undo.

All this will require a very different attitude on the part of Conservative ministers. Instead of 'fighting one's corner', and gaining credit among one's officials by a 'tough' line on demands for reductions in the department budget, the criterion of success must be readiness to cut and cut again. The 'good' Secretary of State for Education will be the one who agrees to reduce the staff/student ratio, increase the size of classes, employ fewer ancillaries and discourage any expenditure on school buildings other than bare necessities. The 'good' Secretary of State for Health and Social Services will be the one who points out to his colleagues that from 1965 to 1973 the number of hospital beds occupied daily fell by 11 per cent and waiting lists grew, while the number of hospital administrative and clerical staff rose by 50 per cent. And illustrations could be multiplied. Getting government off our backs, 'setting these people free', 'a property-owning democracy' — these are admirable Conservative objectives, but they will require hard work, determination and toughness if they are to be achieved. Yet there is no real alternative. The Conservative Party cannot seek the 'middle ground' as it did from 1950 to 1964. The world has changed. There is now no middle ground to seek. Nothing less will suffice than a major reversal of the trends which ever since 1945 Labour has promoted and Conservatives have accepted. There is no other way of reducing taxation and a Conservative Government which cannot achieve that might as well shut up shop.

There is, of course, always the danger that despite the departure of the Grand Chameleon of our times, his successor too may sense the current mood and do something far more drastic than Labour seems ready to do at present. He might actually reduce expenditure instead of promising not to increase it during the next five years by quite as monstrous a figure as he had intended. Thus he might steal the Tory thunder. I do not think that Conservatives should worry unduly. It is seldom a good sign for its prospects when a party in office apes the policy of the opposition. Mr Wilson's 'bonfire of controls' in 1948 did not long precede a massive swing to the right. The Conservative efforts to be 'progressive' in 1963 did not save them in 1964. Peel was said to have stolen the Whigs' clothes when they were bathing. If so, he did them nothing but good. Peel fell in 1846 and for thirty years Britain was dominated by a Whig/Liberal coalition.

2 The Conservative Dilemma

GILLIAN PEELE

At first sight it does not appear very difficult to be a Conservative.
Walter Bagehot, 'Intellectual Conservatism'

It is an unusual period when the Conservative Party collectively sees a need to redefine the principles for which it stands. Traditionally, Tories have distrusted the application of abstract doctrines to politics and have preferred instead to follow the dictates of common sense and experience. Such general questions as the proper relationship between the individual and the State or the nature and purpose of contemporary capitalism have been eschewed as divisive and irrelevant distractions from the search for electoral success; neither the parliamentary party nor the extra-parliamentary organisation have seen much point in debating them either among themselves or even with their opponents. This approach has not meant that the Conservative Party has always been united – in our own century the battles over free trade, the future of India, and the Suez venture were as bitter as any of the Labour Party's 'revisionist' battles of the 1950s – but it has prevented temporary policy disputes from hardening into permanent factions and has enabled the leadership to adapt to new circumstances without the fear that the Party might accuse it of heresy.

Yet such pragmatism, while it undoubtedly has its advantages, has its drawbacks also. Indeed one of the difficulties of arguing the Conservative case is that there is a paucity of reflective writing in the Conservative Party and an absence of magisterial theorists to whom one might turn for inspiration. This is not to say that there have been no thinkers whom Tories have generally admired – Hume, Burke, Disraeli and Oakeshott all adorn the Conservative pantheon – nor to allege that the eloquent personal statements of men such as Lord Hugh Cecil and Lord Hailsham have not been important. It is merely to suggest that within the Conservative Party, because there is no ideological orthodoxy and no equivalent of Karl Marx, there is no tradition of articulating and

13

developing general ideas as opposed to concrete and specific policy proposals.

Scepticism about the role of over-arching theory in politics may thus be seen as something of a mixed blessing from the Conservative Party's point of view. In so far as one of the major objections which Conservatives have to the Socialist philosophy is its dogmatism, the absence of a comprehensive and 'official' statement of beliefs may have been a strength and has certainly saved the party from the charge of hypocrisy. For the Conservative, ordinary men and women and their imperfect and perhaps regrettable wants and emotions have to be seen as the starting-point of political debate and not as the raw material from which a new and radically different sort of society might be moulded. Politics is primarily about the solution of problems which actually manifest themselves, not about the construction of an egalitarian heaven on earth; the role of government should be limited to one that accords with the values of the existing population and not extended in an attempt to fit some *a priori* philosophy or blueprint.

Precisely because the Conservative Party has exhibited such a flexible and pragmatic approach to politics, however, it is all the more important that from time to time it should spell out the fundamentals of its creed as coherently as possible. For, in the absence of such a justification, the critics of the Party will be all too eager to brand tolerant pragmatism as unprincipled opportunism and the merits of the Conservative case will go unheard in the cacophony of ideological encounter. It is vital moreover that in each generation the task of clarification be undertaken afresh. The political battle is never the same for one generation as for the next, if only because politics is a process in which the counters themselves are always changing and, though the Conservative may not want to be the engineer of radical social change nor the witness of a 'moral revolution', he cannot deny that attitudes and outlooks will vary considerably over time. It is imperative therefore that frequent re-examinations of Conservative thinking occur if the Party is not to be burdened with the unreviewed shibboleths of an earlier age and the distinction lost between what should be seen as durable and what as ephemeral. Alexis de Tocqueville criticised the rulers of Europe in the early nineteenth century for being too much concerned with past disputes and too little concerned with anticipating future conflict: ' . . . it is just that to which we give the least attention. Carried away by a rapid current, we obstinately keep our eyes fixed on the ruins still in sight on the bank, while the stream whirls us backward — facing towards the abyss' [*Democracy in America* (1966 edition) p. 6] . The Conservative who indulges his desire to refight battles long since lost pays heavily in terms of his ability to fight battles for which the troops are still preparing.

There will be some periods when a reappraisal of principle and policy on the part of Conservatives will be especially necessary. It is part of the thesis of this book that the mid-1970s constitute such a period in British political life. The reasons for thinking that this is a critical period for our social and political institutions have been examined in some depth both by academic commentators and by the media. Although many of these arguments will be familiar it is perhaps worth restating them since they will undoubtedly be referred to throughout this book. Speaking generally the major premise of these arguments is that the structure and style of British politics is no longer able to cope with the transformed nature of the economic and social life of this country. In this thesis parliamentary democracy — based on the principle of representation through elections — is ill fitted to the movements of power upwards to supranational institutions such as the European Economic Community and multinational corporations and outwards to functionally legitimised groups such as the trade unions and the employers' organisations. Dissatisfaction with government is but a symptom of popular recognition of the fact that power lies not with Westminster or even Whitehall but outside the country altogether — with the Commission or the multinational enterprises or inside the portals of Congress House. The recognition that the institutions of British liberal democracy have lost some of their capacity to control powerful groups inside and outside our society has been compounded by the way in which the country's increasingly dismal economic performance has failed to keep pace with the popular expectations — in part generated by the politicians — of ever-improving living standards.

Specific evidence of this thesis is not hard to find. Indeed looking back over the past ten years of British political debate it is difficult to exaggerate the extent of the collapse in confidence. The widespread dissatisfaction with the two major parties has been reflected both in the growth of minor parties and in particular in Scotland of the Scottish Nationalist Party. Turnout at parliamentary elections has declined substantially since 1945 and the Labour Government elected in October 1974 attained the support of only 39 per cent of those who voted on a turnout of 72 per cent. The electoral system has come under increasing attack, and remedies which even a decade ago would have seemed arcane and alien are being seriously canvassed not merely within the ranks of third-party supporters, but inside the two major parties also. Primaries and proportional representation have many more supporters today than they did ten years ago and the first steps along the road to the public financing of political parties have already been taken. The referendum on the issue of Britain's entry into Europe while allegedly a once-for-all event inevitably raised the question of how far this device might be extended to other matters on which parties were internally divided.

This disintegration of public faith in what was once called the constitution poses a special problem for Conservatives. For they will be inherently suspicious of what may seem new-fangled and foreign remedies and will be perhaps over-sanguine about the merits of the traditional

constitutional framework of unwritten and flexible conventions. Unfortunately an unwritten constitution such as ours which is dependent
upon informal norms cannot operate effectively when there is a sharpening
of political conflict. Heightened inter-party tension immediately threatens
the spirit of self-restraint on which the maintenance of the rules of the
political game are founded. Now it would, I think, be hard to deny that in
the gloomy cycle of inflation and slump, the British political atmosphere
has become charged with ideological hostility and that the goodwill on
which many of the informal constraints were based has evaporated. Once
broken down, goodwill and informal restraint are hard to rebuild and the
Conservative Party finds itself faced with a somewhat stark choice:
between doing nothing in the hope that things will improve and trying
positively to rewrite a constitutional settlement of some kind against a
background of continuing partisan debate. The need to rewrite the
constitutional settlement — which is further explored in Eric Barendt's
chapter — is perhaps the most immediate and unfortunately most intractable problem which Conservatives have to consider in the years ahead.

The disintegration of public faith in the constitution and the sharpening
of political conflict in Britain can be dated from — although not necessarily causally related to — the abandonment of Butskellism as both parties changed their leaders and to some extent their style over the period
1963—5. After the loss of the 1970 election the middle ground was
regarded as a quagmire by the Labour left; and the Heath Government of
1970—4 had too many controversial measures in its programme to make
its claims to that terrain credible. But it was not merely that Government
and Opposition moved away from each other and from consensus policies.
It was also that the establishment of a consensus behind party policies
came to be seen as a dispensable luxury. The primary orientation of both
major political parties to their own activists while in opposition, rather
than to the public at large, and the saddling of the public, through the
doctrine of the mandate, with policies made in opposition has weakened
Governments and weakened Oppositions. It has weakened Governments
because it has made it likely that a Government will spend the first period
of its term of office attempting to wriggle out of foolish commitments
made to appease its own extremists; and it has weakened Oppositions
because criticisms of the Government as they come to be more and
more ideological seem more 'unreasoned' and easier to discount. The
only 'power' which an Opposition in Britain has is the power to persuade
by the quality of its arguments, and if Governments and Oppositions
automatically assume that what the other is saying in the House of
Commons may be ignored, our system of government becomes conducive
to minority tyranny of a frightening kind. No Government need take any
notice of the House of Commons so long as it has an effective majority
and there are no other checks in our systems analogous to those which
Congress and the Supreme Court can exert upon the Presidency in the

American political system. The House of Lords is stymied, particularly in relation to a Labour Government, by the knowledge that any attempt to block the so-called 'popular will' as embodied in the decision of the House of Commons will be to invite the suggestion that the second chamber has outlived its usefulness and that even its residual powers should be taken away. Even on an issue as important to the quality of Britain's political life as the freedom of the press and the closed shop for journalists, the Labour Party did not hesitate to make use of the threat; and in that context it is worth remembering that Edward Short's hints that such obstruction as did occur when the Bill was considered by the Lords would not be tolerated came when Labour had been elected with an overall majority of three and the support of only 39 per cent of the electorate. Such arrogance would be humorous if it did not seem symptomatic of a deep and insidious carelessness of constitutional propriety and popular opinion and a determination to govern as though the majority were of 1945 proportions.

Other examples of the destruction of the bipartisan approach to constitutional matters could be produced without number. The refusal of the 1966—70 Wilson administration to implement the Boundary Commissioners' report, the Labour Party's ambiguous attitude towards the Clay Cross and Shrewsbury picket affairs all reinforce the impression that the Labour Party is unable or unwilling to put constitutional considerations above considerations of party advantage.

The cases of Mr Reginald Prentice, Mr Frank Tomney and others, who although no heroes of the Conservative Party have been persecuted for their views by small and well-organised bands of left-wingers within their constituencies have likewise revealed how vulnerable our system is to infiltration by extremists and how much the landscape of British politics has changed over the past decade. And yet even with this colonisation of the Labour Party by the left wing — which means that a totally unrepresentative group has a major say in the policies and attitudes of a party which as a whole failed to gain the support of a majority of voters — Labour has retained the sympathy if not the votes of men and women who look with horror upon the antics of the Tribune group. That this should be so suggests that the full implications of the internal dynamics of Labour politics have not yet been appreciated fully and that there is a vacuum in British political debate which a party with a determined and subtle leadership must fill.

What is needed to deal with recent developments which have considerably changed the character of British politics then is that at least one major political party should be in a position to mobilise the sentiments and support of the majority of our electors to create a consensus for a new constitutional settlement. For the most part, that majority consists of moderate men and women who deplore many of the recent trends in this country's constitutional development but who have come to see the political process as an occult ritual of interest only to that limited number of citizens who are professionally engaged in it. But to mobilise the moderates in the country in an effort to cut what is admittedly a complex and daunting web of social and economic problems, it is vital that the Conservative Party participates fully in the political and social dialogue which it has too often ignored. Clearly one would not wish the Shadow Cabinet to give up its immediate ambition to replace the Labour Party on the government benches at Westminster, nor does one expect the nation to be transformed overnight into an academic seminar. But we must realise that politics is conducted at a number of levels, not just the level of day-to-day debate in the House of Commons. The Conservative Party cannot afford to fall into the error either of believing that these levels of politics are autonomous; for what has been termed the ideological level — or more graphically the battle of ideas — is sometimes as important in the long run as the battle for victory at the polls.

There are two reasons why the Conservative Party must now take the battle of ideas very seriously indeed. The first is that some theories of how society should be organised are better than others. It has become fashionable for instance to suggest that there is little difference between the direct control exercised over the media in a dictatorship and the indirect influence which capitalist owners can exert in a liberal democracy. If we are so tolerant as to allow such ideas to flourish without rebuttal, then we do society and freedom a grave disservice. The second reason for castigating the tendency of the Conservative Party to neglect general ideas is that the intellectual climate cannot be divorced from the more practical and ostensibly limited process of policy-making. It affects the success with which such policies can be implemented. Even the discussion of the most bread-and-butter issues of politics takes place against a background of assumptions and generally held ideas; and by attempting to mould, or at least prevent the distortion of, that intellectual milieu a party is contributing to the next generation's capacity to pursue certain strategies or policies.

Consider for example the failure of Mr Heath's Government in the field of industrial relations. Here the Conservative Party was acting in a way which in the eyes of trade union leaders threatened their entrenched interests and their rights. From the point of view of the Conservative Government, however, all that the Industrial Relations Act was doing was ending the extra-legal position of a powerful pressure group. Although the Conservative Party assumed that the full force of the union movement and the Labour Party would be ranged against the Industrial Relations Bill while it was being considered by Parliament, the Party also assumed that there existed sufficient respect for the established democratic procedures to ensure that once the Bill became law it would be obeyed even if not liked. This analysis ignored the fact that a substantial section of the trade union movement considered that its primary obligation was to defend the interests of the members rather than the principles of the rule of law. In other words in any clash of legitimacies — i.e. any conflict of authority between representation based on the national electoral system expressed through Parliament and representation based on class and theoretically expressed through the trade unions — the authority of Parliament would be defied. The Conservative Government's assumptions also ignored the fact that so greatly had the climate of opinion changed since the early 1960s that members of the Labour Party in Parliament would with varying degrees of enthusiasm encourage and approve resistance to the 1971 Act and would disregard the argument that our system of government can only survive if there is respect for the rule of law on the part of both government and opposition. Instead Michael Foot adopted the rhetoric of Marxist analysis which portrays the law as the embodiment of class rule and attacked not merely the Government for introducing the legislation — which he was of course perfectly entitled to do — but also the judges for administering it.

If this situation is compared with the United States where legislation to regulate labour relations is often mooted and sometimes passed, it can be seen that while the unions there will do what they can to prevent such measures from reaching the statute book or will actively work to repeal, for example, section 14b of the Taft-Hartley Act, the law is generally complied with once it is passed. The United States in fact may have a more deeply ingrained respect for the legal and constitutional processes in its national political culture than we have on this side of the Atlantic, whatever else may be at fault in the American system. In short then the Tory mistake in 1971 was that the Government did not fully understand that the values upon which it was relying to secure acceptance of its controversial legislation were not present in the leaders of the group it wished to regulate. And more significantly, perhaps, these values did not appear very salient to the people who were influencing public opinion about the scope and nature of the legislation — the journalists and television commentators, teachers and lecturers who all contributed to the debate.

A second example of the potential importance of the battle of ideas is the present discussion about the choice between those policies which seek to maximise the individual's cash wage — i.e. the money left in his pocket after tax — and policies which seek to maximise the so-called social wage — the services provided for the community as a whole which are provided regardless of the individual's desire for them in that form. The Conservative Party would clearly like to shift the balance back towards cash wage maximising policies. But — and it is a very big but — the lesson of the Industrial Relations Act is pertinent here. The Tories must not overlook the fact that the general population is not identical to the section of the party which assembles at Blackpool or some other seaside resort to cheer such sentiments. The assumptions of the social wage provision have become deeply ingrained not only in a large section of the electorate —

which has remained curiously ignorant of the fact that indirectly these services still have to be financed — but also among those groups who with little exaggeration may be said to constitute the country's unacknowledged legislators: the critics and commentators, experts and publicists, who directly or indirectly make up what is called 'informed public opinion' and who have a substantial capacity to affect the way the man in the street evaluates governmental action. A government which legislated contrary to those values without carefully preparing its ground would do so at its peril.

Such an analysis of the reception which legislation running contrary to *étatist* values might expect to receive must sound gloomy; but I do not by any means want to suggest that government should never try to alter public opinion by legislation or that a move towards giving the individual citizen greater control over his income or restructing the framework of industrial relations will always be politically impossible. What I am emphasising is the care which a party wanting to introduce such changes must take to see that it has prepared the ground for them. Certainly, at the very least it must ensure that the principles on which such policy changes are based are well understood and that there is sympathy with those principles somewhere in the groups which form opinion and dominate the means of communication. And that process of laying the ground for change takes time, which is why it is imperative that the Conservative Party needs to be able to sustain intellectual debate about the country's political values beyond the life-span of a single Parliament. It is simply no use introducing radical legislation such as the Industrial Relations Act and then hoping, when difficulties are encountered, that the issues which it raised will go away. If it was worth incurring hostility for the Act in the first place there must surely be something to be said for continuing the debate about the principles inherent in it. Similarly, however obvious the cause of 'national unity' may have been to the party hierarchy in October 1974, it was sprung upon the unsuspecting public with all the artistry of the Sorcerer's Apprentice and removed with approximately the same amount of skill. Some of the ideas inherent in that campaign were worth following through but, sadly, they have been forgotten in the absorption with the leadership change and the exigencies of short-term politics.

Throughout this essay I have referred to certain groups as 'opinion-forming groups' without perhaps offering a precise definition of what exactly they are and how they distil political ideas. By 'opinion-forming groups' I mean those individuals who have the capacity and the opportunity to influence public values in any way, be they university or school teachers, clerics or authors, television producers or leader-writers. The Conservative Party's position in relation to these groups has generally been one of mutual suspicion. For the Parliamentary Party and some of the Party's leaders have often been contemptuous of 'clever men' (one has only to read George Orwell's *The Lion and the Unicorn* to get the flavour of the antagonism between these groups in the inter-war period) and in return it has been something of the mark of Cain to be known as a Conservative in the worlds of academe and the media. The unhappy result of this division has been a certain isolation of the Parliamentary Party from its sympathisers in these other spheres and that isolation has made the Party look rather more like the coalition of economic interests so often caricatured by our opponents. But there is now a sign that things are changing: the unthinking Socialism of the sixties no longer dominates the university world, although it would be wrong to see this as necessarily leading to an increase in the number of card-carrying Conservative Party members there. What the dissolution of the Socialist orthodoxy should produce, however, is a change in the intellectual climate which is of course precisely what the country needs if it is to be jerked out of those habits of mind which are destroying both its material prosperity and the quality of life in Britain generally. It is vital that the Conservative Party be able to create and nourish that change and that it makes itself able to call upon the talents and sympathies of all those who share the Party's values rather than those of its opponents. The Conservative Party has in short to be able to transcend the perhaps limited sphere of partisan politics and make common cause with all those who share a belief in the virtues of our society and the values of a liberal democracy.

What are the values which the Conservative feels are endangered and which he should set about building a national consensus to support? How far can we go towards producing a Conservative philosophy which will be appropriate to a society marked by rapid social change? The values which I as a Conservative wish to preserve are the principles of pluralism and I want to suggest that it is by exploring the implications of that difficult term that Conservatives may be able to find the somewhat delicate balance between scepticism and faith which is inherent in the Conservative cast of mind. There is an enormous literature on pluralism as a concept of political analysis and it cannot of course provide a complete answer to all the questions which one might like to see covered in a discussion of political fundamentals. Nevertheless it seems to me that as an approach to politics it offers the most satisfactory alternative to the socialist model of society and the state.

There will of course be Conservatives for whom the idea of a pluralist society will be far too liberal in conception and who would prefer to advocate a political philosophy based securely upon some fundamental notion of religious truth or purpose. The implications of the pluralist creed are in short likely to offend many who see Conservatism as standing much more for the organic and perhaps theistically sanctioned social order than for the dynamic and neutral tension of the pluralist state. And there is much to be said for believing that a society united by religious belief (or as Tocqueville thought by patriotism) will be more cohesive than one where there are few shared ultimate values. However, it is doubtful whether the process of secularisation and the accompanying decline of a common morality can be reversed, however much many Conservatives would wish it otherwise. If the choice is then between a common purpose provided by one of the new religions of political salvation and accepting the fact that no such communality of values exists, Conservatives should unhesitatingly opt for the latter alternative.

The basis of what I shall call pluralism is then that our knowledge of temporal things is limited, incomplete and hypothetical and that moral beliefs are necessarily subjective. Any theory which purports to be a complete explanation of man's being in the world or to be valid for all times has therefore to be rejected if it claims to be anything other than metaphysical. In other words we should view with extreme scepticism any claim that a given political system such as Marxism-Leninism is founded on scientific principles and we should hold at the back of our minds the awareness that even the most cherished social beliefs and theories may one day have to be discarded.

Given the hypothetical basis of our knowledge about the world and given that we cannot scientifically justify any single theory of how a political system ought to be organised, we cannot be justified in imposing our moral beliefs upon others however convinced we ourselves may be of their truth or utility.

Similarly we ought to proceed with caution in any attempt to improve our current institutional framework. There will always be occasions on which the politician or administrator is called upon to improve some ailing institution or to accommodate some new demand. Indeed it has been argued here that we need to improve upon our present constitutional arrangements in what may seem to some a quite new and radical manner. But what we must never forget is that in politics there is no obvious truth with a capital T which we are entitled to implement and no political remedy which is not inherently an experiment. The adoption of such an attitude does not mean that we should eschew change. We should on the contrary be as sceptical of our existing institutions' ability to monopolise wisdom and efficiency as we are of our own ability to replace them with anything better. But it does mean that we should not set up in business as merchants of rational reform nor go around peddling solutions to problems which we have ourselves created by coming to the market place with too inflated a vision of the goods which we have to sell. Where there is sustained and widespread dissatisfaction with the arrangements of a society then of course it is proper to see if they can be improved. But the attempt at improvement must be made in the knowledge that we may make things worse rather than better and that, if possible, we should not block the way to other alternative solutions, nor even to a return to previous arrangements.

The caution which the Conservative Party ought to show in relation to its own or indeed any party's ability to greatly improve upon the condition of society is linked to what is for me the most important principle of pluralism: that the polity ought to encourage the largest amount of diversity and variety consonant with the maintenance of law and order. The impossibility of proving that any single idea, belief or theory is universally true will obviously make us want to preserve the free circulation of opinions and to resist attempts to impede this circulation however well intentioned the motive. A pluralist society is one where competing hypotheses and theories can be tested against each other quite freely and it is this which makes us want to guard the institutions of communication from domination by any single opinion or faction and makes us wish to resist the use of government censorship and the growth of conformity of opinion. It is this which leads us to insist that our institutions of education – especially our universities – should not become places where what is studied is dependent upon the needs of government or industry, the demands of ideologues or even, within limits, the constraints of public expenditure. And it is this belief which ought to make Conservatives – although they have not always been as quick to take up such causes as they should have been – hostile to any attempt to extend or reinforce our Official Secrets Act, pornography legislation, D notices and our stringent defamation laws.

This intellectual pluralism, which has clear implications at the level of our society's arrangements with regard to civil liberties, has other implications for the State. Pluralism entails a recognition of the legitimacy, not merely of a wide variety of moral goals and political creeds which may exist in a society, but also of a wide variety of life-styles and of group and associational activity, much of which may run counter to the preferences of the Government of the day. The State – by which is meant the institutions of central government – must recognise the legitimacy of such variety and must define the task of government as being to provide the conditions in which such activity may flourish and prosper auto-nomously rather than always feeling that it should orchestrate and harmonise it. In this context it is to be hoped that devolution if and when it does occur may do something to reverse the dominance in our political system of the twin evils of centralisation and uniformity. Tolerance of diversity is one of the greatest advantages of a diffusion of power, but the political habits which we have acquired in the recent past may make genuine decentralisation a much more difficult exercise than anyone originally envisaged.

The most obvious sphere where the specifically pluralist approach to society differs from that of the Labour Party and other adherents of Socialist or quasi-Socialist creeds is the economy. For the Socialist the institutions of private enterprise are suspect because they are seen as the concrete manifestations of the urge towards profit in human nature and because they impede progress towards the goal of a fully egalitarian society. However much Socialists revise their creed to allow the private sector to continue in being, the mixed economy will always be based in their eyes on a somewhat immoral process of exploitation. The preference of the Socialist, it seems fair to say, is almost always for the centrally planned economy; and his commitment to private industry and enterprise is necessarily weak. For the pluralist on the other hand it is fundamental that the State should not be allowed to assume a monopoly in the economic sphere and that as far as possible the private sector of industry and commerce should be the dominant force in the polity's economic life. The pluralist does not, however, see this as fundamental because he believes capitalism to be necessarily good in itself. He desires the prosperity of the private sector because he fears that otherwise the State will become so powerful as to choke and suffocate all other private institutions and activities whether economic or not and will ultimately forbid any organisation to compete with it. To say that a country cannot afford to let its system of private enterprise die is not to say that there is no role for the State in the economy nor is it to assert that the operations of business and financial organisations will always be free from flaws. But it is to assert very strongly that the alternative of complete State regulation has consequences far beyond the arena of economic activity.

The Conservative Party has a somewhat ambiguous history in relation to capitalism. In the nineteenth century it was the Liberal Party rather than the Conservative Party which was against control and regulation of the economy by government; the Disraelian Tory Party, on both paternalistic and pragmatic grounds, did not set its face dogmatically against State intervention. Of late, however, the Party has become not merely the champion of private enterprise, in contrast with the increasing threat to it from the Labour Party, but has experienced what one commentator has called a flirtation with neo-capitalism. Neo-capitalism may be said to take the sanctity of the market as its starting point and sees the price mechanism as the panacea for all social ills. Consequently there are arguments in the creed which attempt to justify the reintroduction of the market into areas such as health, housing and education or to extend its sphere there. Up to a point such a movement is a healthy antidote to the ever-extending arm of bureaucratic control and the soporific values which come with that extension of the role of the State. It is however dangerous to lose sight of the fact that capitalism can throw up practices, such as monopolies, as unacceptable as those of the State and that it too can be lethargic and inefficient. Thus there may from time to time be a need for control and intervention. The point which Conservatives must emphasise is that the existence of many industries and producers usually prevents the situation from getting out of hand, for even if the competition is not 'perfect' there is usually some discipline operating upon firms which need to satisfy the consumer rather than, as is the case with the nationalised industries, no discipline at all. In the case of the State no such discipline need or would exist unless there were an alternative set of institutions operating in direct competition with it and whose practices could be cited as examples in any criticism of the State's performance.

The argument against monopoly holds good in other areas apart from the economy. It is sound and important to the pluralist in areas where we have been encouraged to think of the State as the fount of all wisdom, logic and material provision. Obviously the debate about whether the country's private education institutions should be allowed to continue or whether the State should try to abolish private medical treatment are also instances of fields in which the pluralist will have to give a clear and forceful answer. Whatever the dangers from inequalities of access to private education or medicine — and it would be foolish to deny that such inequality has consequences for society as a whole — the pluralist believes that the danger to the quality of society from a State monopoly of these services is much greater. It would be more dangerous because there could be no guarantees about the quality of the services the State would provide; dangerous because an impoverishing homogeneity would be forced upon us by the removal of skilled persons from our society who would not necessarily transfer their talents to the public domain; and dangerous because we would be contributing towards a massive inequality of power in society by granting yet further authority to a bureaucracy and a political élite free from control, criticism and accountability.

There is one monopoly which the State does have, of course, and which it must retain, and that is the monopoly of coercion. The State's role in a plural society is clearly to provide the basic necessity of civil peace and to encourage what might be called reciprocal restraint on the part of groups and individuals. Not everyone in a society can get what they want all the time, and at any given time there is bound to be an imbalance between certain groups and forces some of whom will prove better manipulators of the system than others. The State therefore — which can claim to speak for society as a whole from time to time — does have the right to intervene to restore the balance between forces and groups and to act, as an American economist would perhaps put it, as a 'countervailing power'. The problem is to ensure that politicians do actually speak for society as a whole when they intervene and are not in the process of forcing society into a mould of their own choosing with the aid of an increasingly powerful bureaucracy. The task of the politician is in part therefore to persuade groups and individuals placed in positions of temporary advantage not to exploit that position for purely sectional ends and to attempt themselves to keep a balance between the competition of demands and interests generated by a plural society. The task is not of course an easy one; a course must be charted between imposing a subjective view on the public regardless of its popularity and being unduly influenced by those groups already exerting power in a country. It is probably not a balance which can ever be got completely right. But if the State takes an increasingly partisan role in the struggle it is almost certain that it will be got completely wrong.

The philosophy of pluralism, I have suggested, is a strand which runs through much Conservative thinking and provides a starting-point for resisting the attacks of more aggressively ideological opponents. It has also some implications for the future development of Conservative policy. First the Party must ensure that it never becomes the prisoner of any single interest or faction. It has in short to remain a broad-based catch-all party as it has always tried to be in the past. Secondly, although the current concern with economic policy is understandable in a period when the country's financial predicament is gloomy, the Party must not fall into the trap of seeing economic doctrine as the touchstone of all political truths. Thirdly the Party must pay a great deal more attention to the problem of communicating the values of pluralism than it has done in the past. The extension of the scope of State activity has brought with it perhaps a corresponding decline in the virtues of individualism and diversity as outlined here and a corresponding torpor in those sections of society which depend most heavily upon them. What Tocqueville called the mania for centralisation has convinced even Conservatives at times that the State necessarily knows best and that disagreement about policies and priorities is unacceptable. As Conservatives we must show more imagination in areas where it would be possible to increase diversity and competition, and we must avoid arguments which would not be out of place in our opponents' mouths.

The fourth and final lesson for the Conservative Party is that its case is not one which need appeal exclusively to paid-up Conservatives. We have a focal point around which we should elaborate our message and an intellectually respectable creed which ought to make us the natural choice of moderate men and women in this country. The party faces the task of mobilising that natural majority. It is in everyone's interests that it should do so.

3 Constitutional Reforms

ERIC BARENDT

Conservatives have never been very interested in constitutional reform. They have shown even less enthusiasm for reform of the electoral system. Priding themselves upon their pragmatism, they are usually dogmatic about the virtues of the British constitution and the two-party system. Quintin Hogg's classic statement of Conservative philosophy, *The Case for Conservatism* [Penguin Books, 1947, revised edition 1959], discusses maternity benefits and the Metropolitan Water Board, but contains no critical examination of the nation's major constitutional and political institutions. Defence of 'the constitution' has indeed long been a fundamental Tory principle, despite occasional lapses such as Bonar Law's support of the resistance in Ulster to the Home Rule Bill in 1912. Moreover, the maintenance of existing institutions was one of the three principles declared by Disraeli in the famous Crystal Palace speech. With authority such as this, who needs argument?

Now, however, after two electoral defeats in a year and with the prospect of a period of opposition, Conservatives are seriously questioning – in some cases for the first time – aspects of the constitution and electoral system. There are sound practical reasons for much of this unusual cerebration: how can the Nationalist tide, particularly in Scotland, be stemmed? Would a system of proportional representation have prevented the formation of the Labour Government, or at least restrained its zeal for Socialist measures? Would a Bill of Rights help to preserve the fundamental freedoms which Conservatives see as endangered by Socialist government? Many Conservatives are, however, uneasy about the propriety of these speculations; after all, they are hardly compatible with traditional Tory reverence for the unique merits of the British constitution. But I suspect Disraeli would have approved, particularly as it may involve stealing a few Liberal clothes! And it may be argued that in any case it is time Conservatives rethought their attitudes to these matters.

It is important first to appreciate the nature of the developments which necessitate this reappraisal. This century has witnessed a massive extension of the functions and powers of central government; administrations grow larger and the number of civil servants has increased tenfold. The ability of the House of Commons to control the Executive has declined with the tightening of party discipline; and even if they had the will, Members of

27

Parliament often lack the information and expertise necessary to confront the Government on equal terms. At the same time many powers of local government have been taken away from it and have been transferred to central government or unelected *ad hoc* bodies, such as the Gas and Electricity Boards and the regional health and water authorities. The significance of these changes was stated in the Memorandum of Dissent to the Kilbrandon Report on the Constitution [Cmnd 5460–1, 1973, at paragraph 26]: 'The fundamental consequence of these trends has been the erosion of the extent to which we as people govern ourselves.'

In the last few years it has been possible to detect a decline in the respect for Parliament and the institutions of government generally, surely partly attributable to the developments just described. There is more frequently than before recourse to direct action and the politics of protest; correspondingly there is more apathy at elections, particularly for local government. Membership of the political parties has declined, and there is increasing disbelief in the ability of politicians of all parties to solve the felt problems of the day. Ultimately at issue may be what is sometimes referred to as the question of 'legitimacy' – the entitlement of our institutions to respect, and their laws to obedience. The fact that these anxieties have been voiced on previous occasions should not make us complacent. The probability is that the problem will become more acute, as governments, either for ideological reasons or under the pressure of events, take on more responsibility for the direction of affairs. This is more likely to be the case under Labour Governments, naturally inclined to seek centralised and total solutions to economic and social problems. But the experience of the last Conservative Government with regard to the Industrial Relations Act and the Housing Finance Act shows that the left has already raised questions about (or exploited the issue of) the legitimacy of laws.

The conventional response of Conservatives to these difficulties is a vigorous reassertion of the rule of law. This is certainly not to be despised, not at any rate by a lawyer, but I doubt whether it is good enough now. It is easy to appreciate the orthodox response from an historical perspective. In both the nineteenth and this century, the Conservative Party has stood for authority and order. At first these values, necessary for the preservation of organised society, were defended against the more extreme forms of liberalism, which emphasised the fundamental liberties of the individual and denied the state more than a minimal role. So Conservatives have consistently rejected J. S. Mill's proposition that the only rightful exercise of power by the State over an individual is to prevent him harming another. Authority was associated with a strong, central government and the constitutional doctrine that Parliament is sovereign. Order is reconciled with liberty by the influence of the common law and by the restraints imposed by the British tradition of tolerance. Since during the nineteenth century both parties shared this tradition of tolerant political behaviour, Conservatives had no need to worry about potential losses of liberty, whichever party was in office. With Gladstonian Liberals on the benches opposite, the paternalist element in Conservative thought naturally predominated. Though it is fifty years since the Liberals last provided serious political opposition, Conservatives still feel it necessary to assert that they are the party of authority. So *The Case for Conservatism* was as much concerned to repudiate the Liberal heresy as it was the Socialist threat.

In this century the challenge to established authority has largely come from the Labour Party and the trade union wing of the Labour movement. Against this the Conservative response has again been to assert the rule of law. Sometimes this has been achieved simply enough by direct legislation, as after the General Strike of 1926 (though this was subsequently repealed by the Attlee Government). More recently Baldwin's desire that the Labour movement should be converted to constitutional and legal patterns of behaviour has been satisfied for the most part. Even the Tribune group is fully in favour of working for radical social change within the existing Parliamentary system.

Paradoxically, however, this is now the cause of the Conservatives' difficulty. Labour Governments, committed to a Socialist programme, realise that much can be accomplished by legislation and lawful administrative fiat. Conservatives, accustomed this century to being the 'natural' governing party and to sharing in a tradition of political restraint, have only recently woken up to the fact that the freedoms they cherish may lawfully be taken away from them. Against this spectre, the cry of 'rule of law' will avail them nothing. Furthermore, beguiled by the fact that the Executive acts in the name of the Crown, with all its sentimental associations, they have never been too troubled by the processes and ever-increasing powers of government. Faced by a bureaucratic Socialist Government this complacency can no longer be justified and maintained.

At long last it is the libertarian element in Conservative thought which is being emphasised. Questions are rightly being asked about the appropriate level of government intervention in and control of economic activity. They might also be asked about our governmental institutions and processes. Should the power of central government be broken up by devolution to Scotland, Wales and the English regions? Should government be less secret and subject to more control through a Bill of Rights? Would the authority of, and the respect for, Parliament be enhanced by proportional representation? These are vital issues. Only if the right solutions are found may it be possible to avoid the crisis which would arise when the legitimacy of government is widely questioned. The temptation of the Socialists faced by a recalcitrant population would be to move in more authoritarian directions. There is no alternative in their ideology.

Conservatives would surely prefer to remove this danger by well-ordered constitutional reform — reform designed to limit the powers of government and puncture its intolerable arrogance.

Despite the result of the debate at the Party Conference in October 1975, it seems relatively clear that Conservatives will be discussing electoral reform with some seriousness throughout their period in opposition. Whether this will continue to be the case if they are returned at the next election with a clear majority is less certain! The temptation to drop the subject, particularly if (as may be anticipated) the Liberals do badly at the polls, will be virtually irresistible. Nevertheless, it should perhaps be resisted. At the moment of victory it will be easy to forget that the Labour Party will have a sporting chance of winning the following election, and that it is likely to be more doctrinaire on that occasion than before. It may be defeatist, as Angus Maude has contended, not to believe that the Conservatives will win next time; it might on the other hand be thought foolish to ignore the possibility that some day another Labour Government will be returned under the present electoral system.

For the Liberal Party the desirability of proportional representation — in some form or other — seems, of course, a matter of fairness. Conservatives need not look at it in this way, though they might make themselves a little more congenial if they did not so often appear complacent about the present system's arguable injustices. After the February election in 1974, when the Labour Government was returned in spite of the fact that it obtained fewer popular votes than the Conservatives, this attitude may have become less common. Nevertheless, some rather dubious arguments are being used against the introduction of any system of proportional representation, of which the Single Transferable Vote (STV) is probably the best. [The various methods of electoral reform are discussed in *Adversary Politics and Electoral Reform*, essays edited by S. E. Finer (Anthony Wigram, 1975).] One or two of these arguments emerged in the debate in April 1975 in the House of Lords [H.L., vol. 359, cols 897ff.] ; a common one, used frequently by spokesmen of both major parties, is that multi-member constituencies under the STV system would lead to a weaker relationship between electorate and member. There is something in this, but surely it is of comparatively little relevance when the issue is the most desirable method of representing political opinion in Parliament. Adherents of the argument are giving undue emphasis to the traditional aspects of an MP's role and ignore contemporary reality. The redress of constituents' grievances is now often best secured, in any case, by other means, e.g. the Parliamentary Commissioner. Some Members are now discouraged from continuing a political career by the intolerable pressures of combining national political and constituency work. Multi-member constituencies might enable some

Members to concentrate on the larger, national issues, while others devoted more of their energies to constituents' problems.

A much more formidable objection to proportional representation is said to be that it would remove the electorate's right to choose the government at the polls. As PR would almost inevitably lead to substantial representation for all three British parties (with perhaps a large number of Nationalists and others being returned), the Government would be formed instead by bargaining between the parties. Either a coalition or some other informal agreement of support would result. This is considered to be undemocratic, or less democratic than the present system. But there is no obvious democratic or, more important, fair solution where, say, 40 per cent of the electorate vote for one party, 38 per cent for a second, and 22 per cent for the third. Propositions about 'the power of the electorate to choose governments' smack of Rousseau's 'General Will', and sound odd, to say the least, on Tory lips. In any case, as has been frequently pointed out, all parties are themselves coalitions, and there seems nothing intrinsically different about bargaining *between* parties with regard to government policies and the bargaining which at present occurs *inside* them. Moreover, the attitude of minor parties to prospective coalitions or less formal support agreements will generally be determined during the election campaign, as happens at the moment in West Germany, the Republic of Ireland and in other countries where proportional representation obtains.

The specific Conservative anxiety is that proportional representation would lead to perpetual Labour-Liberal government of the character which has governed Sweden for the last few decades: the Conservatives would be doomed, it is said, to permanent opposition. This calculation is probably too pessimistic. It seems odd to weigh it more heavily in the scales than the comparative certainty under the present system of the existence from time to time of minority, unchecked Labour Governments. If the present Labour Government had had to depend on Liberal support, there would have been no Community Land Act, no Industry Act, no Trade Union and Labour Relations (Amendment) Act, no nationalisation of North Sea oil, no Dock Work Regulation Act, and no indemnity for the Clay Cross councillors; and there might perhaps have been earlier action on wage inflation. This is not an exhaustive list of the evils which might have been avoided. Of course in different times the Liberal leopard might change its spots, but not if it wished to draw on and expand its present support.

The Conservative fear is often put in another way: there would be less likelihood of unchecked Conservative government. This is true, and it would be dishonest not to admit it. The next Conservative Government may want to take tough and radical decisions, particularly in the economic sphere, which would not be practicable in the more subtle world of coalition politics. But in the long run Conservatives, who are naturally sceptical, should be almost as suspicious of their own party's claim to a monopoly of wisdom as those made by the other parties. In politics it is probably more important to prevent evil than to attempt to realise good. This is rarely appreciated nowadays by Conservatives, which only shows how, as Professor Oakeshott would put it, the 'rationalist' mentality — with all its pet schemes and manifesto projects — has gripped them. Resistance to evil can easily be accomplished from within a coalition, but more ambitious plans might in that context have to be abandoned.

Lastly, opponents of proportional representation contend that all coalitions are weak and indecisive. The argument that British government is not strong enough is now a familiar one, though its proponents could probably only point to the National Union of Mineworkers as an example of a victorious adversary. The underlying weakness of British government is even made the theme of the opening chapter of Ian Gilmour's *The Body Politic* [Hutchinson 1969, revised 1971], entitled 'Where has all the power gone?'. It is important, however, to be clear about what exactly this weakness is. The failures of the British government of the time to rearm before the last war or, if we may take but one more recent example, to apply earlier for admission to the EEC, are not indications of the absence of central power; rather they indicate a lack of courage, or plain stupidity. British governments do appear to have enough strength, but it is the strength of blundering elephants: we might reasonably prefer such animals to be weaker. We would certainly wish them more intelligent. From comparative experience, say of the Scandinavian countries or West Germany, it appears that coalitions govern coherently and decisively, and in the light of our own recent history we might with some reason expect them to perform better than single party administrations. In addition, more and more people, particularly in industry, would welcome the comparative continuity of approach of coalition governments.

This part of the essay has not been concerned to emphasise the positive merits of the Single Transferable Vote — for example, the choice the electorate would then have between candidates from the same party; rather its purpose is to attempt to allay some Conservative fears about electoral reform. If the Labour Party was to become in perpetuity a Social Democrat party, barely distinguishable from the present Liberals, electoral reform would not be worth the trouble. But the risk of Socialism, introduced on the basis of a 40 per cent vote and the silly (and, as currently interpreted, vicious) doctrine of the mandate is a great one to run. Parliament, on which the survival of the Government depends, is not fully representative of the people; too little attempt is made by the Party ideologues to compromise and to adjust to the general public climate of opinion, for the system offers them no inducement to do so.

Criticism of our present electoral system and the style of government it seems frequently to encourage is becoming more widespread. Conservatives should at least attempt to understand this phenomenon and engage in dispassionate argument about the merits of the various proposals made for reform. There are sound practical reasons for this exercise. There will be more Conservatives in the proposed Scottish Assembly under a system of PR than under the present electoral system, the continued use of which might lead to the absolute and final demise of the Conservative Party in Scotland. Secondly, there will be some pressure to introduce a system of proportional representation for the direct elections to the European Assembly projected for 1978. The next Conservative Government then might seriously contemplate some measure of electoral reform.

If the Conservatives are undecided about electoral reform, at least they are probably relatively clear about the arguments on both sides. This is less evident with regard to the current debate on devolution where the Conservative contribution so far has been about as garbled (and guarded) as that of a schoolboy who has not done his prep. This is surprising in a way, for there has been ample time for the exercise; the Kilbrandon Royal Commission was set up as long ago as 1969. But to be fair, few people anticipated its proposals, or more crucially, the continuing success of the Scottish (and, to a much lesser extent, the Welsh) Nationalists. Only the political decline of the Nationalist parties could now take devolution off the political agenda, and despite their apparent setback in the EEC Referendum, this does not appear at all likely. (Why should not the Celts opt to be Nationalist and European?) The present Government's proposals for devolution in the White Paper of November 1975 [*Our Changing Democracy*, Cmnd 6348] have done nothing to placate Nationalist demands; on the contrary, all the signs are that the White Paper has provided them with more ammunition for electoral battles. It is now imperative for Conservatives to clarify their position — if only to avoid further electoral losses in Scotland, where their fortunes declined so rapidly in 1974.

For the purposes of this discussion it is worth recalling briefly the disagreement between the majority of the Kilbrandon Commission and the signatories of the Memorandum of Dissent. An analysis of this divergence might enable Conservatives to see the 'devolution question' in its proper perspective. The majority took the view that there was significant spontaneous popular demand for devolution in Scotland and Wales as a means of improving the quality of government in those parts of the United Kingdom. The dissenters, however, found that discontent with the working of government, in particular with the inadequate extent of popular participation, was equally widespread throughout the country; in response to specific questions about the desirability of more regional government, the replies in Scotland and Wales did not show more enthusiasm for devolution than those given in the English regions. I suspect that the explanation is this. The minority on the Commission are right in their finding that there is general dissatisfaction with the operation and processes of government. The survey undertaken by the Commission did not show any significant regional variations in this attitude. But in Scotland, and to some extent Wales, this discontent is spontaneously channelled into a demand for national independence, or at least more self-government. Alienation from government (coupled in Scotland with the discovery of oil) has reawakened the dormant, but ancient, nationalist aspirations of the Scots and Welsh. Thus, though at one level the country merely faces the problem of re-emergent nationalism, this should be seen also as an aspect of the question of the legitimacy of government discussed earlier in this chapter. A solution attempted in terms of nationalism alone may well not meet the real problems disclosed in the Memorandum of Dissent.

As has been frequently emphasised in both the Parliamentary and national debate, the real problem is what to do about devolution in England. The present proposals of the Labour Government will result in a blatantly unequal treatment of the different parts of the United Kingdom. Scotland (though not Wales) will have its own legislative assembly with power to make laws over such fields as housing and education, and yet it will continue to send a disproportionately large number of Members of Parliament to Westminster — among other things to vote on specifically English matters. This situation cannot possibly be justified, and intolerable strains would no doubt occur if the allegiance of the Scottish Members was to be decisive in determining the composition of the United Kingdom Government. The truth is, though regrettably few have had the insight or courage to say it, that devolution for Scotland and Wales entails devolution for England as well — a perception, incidentally, which did not escape Campbell-Bannerman a hundred years ago. [See John Wilson, *A Life of Sir Henry Campbell-Bannerman* (Constable, 1973) p. 155.]

The co-existence of an English and a United Kingdom Parliament, both presumably sitting in London, would be bizarre. England is so much the largest part of the country that its representatives would dominate the United Kingdom Parliament. The best approach would be devolution to a number of English regions, perhaps based, as Ian Gilmour suggested in *The Body Politic* [p. 332], on the economic planning regions. There are two obvious objections to this course, quite apart from the difficulties of determining which powers should be devolved from the United Kingdom Parliament: first, there is no apparent substantial demand for regional devolution in England; and secondly, it would add yet another layer of government to the existing three. The problem exists largely because of the Conservatives' own Local Government Act of 1972, a really unfortunate measure which is rightly held partly responsible for the huge increase in spending by local government. The creation of a fourth tier of government would understandably be resented. It is indeed tragic that the Conservatives' short-sightedness in reforming local government without regard for the devolution question now hinders them from offering coherent solutions to this present constitutional difficulty.

Another unsatisfactory aspect of the Kilbrandon proposals, which has received relatively little comment, concerns the relationship between the United Kingdom Parliament and Government and the proposed regional assemblies. Quite apart from the revenue difficulties – are Scotland and Wales to have powers of taxation? – there is the delicate question whether the Westminster Parliament should have power to disallow regional legislation. The solution suggested in the Kilbrandon Report and now proposed in the 1975 White Paper is that it should have such power in law, but that by convention it should rarely be exercised. It is hard to disagree with a distinguished constitutional lawyer who has observed: 'It is remarkable that such an interaction of law and convention should be contemplated in advance for an entirely new system of government, and in making its forecast the Commission came perilously close to proposing federal government without the courage of its convictions. . . . A federal plan would be a more honest plan. [D. G. T. Williams in *Devolution*, essays edited by Prof. H. Calvert (Professional Books Ltd, 1975) pp. 72 and 76.] This insight that any effective degree of devolution really entails a federal solution has been appreciated by at least one Conservative Member of Parliament, Alex Fletcher [H.C., vol. 885, col. 1252].

Conservatives, as Mr Whitelaw observed in the House of Commons debate on devolution in February 1975, are traditionally committed to preservation of the Union and are, therefore, reluctant to contemplate any radical constitutional change. But Conservatives should not be over-influenced by the sentimental legacies of constitutional history, and should not forget that a more important element in their thought is a passionate opposition to centralised bureaucracy and the concentration of power. For this reason, as Malcolm Rifkind, MP, has contended [*Crossbow*, August 1975, pp. 10–11], Conservatives should welcome the prospect of devolution. This means that the Conservative opposition to the forthcoming Bill should endeavour to ensure the maximum practicable devolution of powers to the Scottish and Welsh Assemblies, and should vigorously oppose the envisaged reserve powers of the Westminster Government, which can only create tension and conflict. A genuine devolution of power to all parts of the United Kingdom – still more, of course, the unthinkable federal solution – would break up the growing monopoly of Whitehall; and it might reverse the decline in democratic control and local autonomy which has been such a marked feature of political development since the last war.

Although relatively radical in its devolution proposals, the Kilbrandon Commission was cautious in its observations on a Bill of Rights. It observed that though there were merits in Bills of Rights, there were difficulties to recommending them as limitations on the powers of the proposed regional assemblies. The task of adjudicating in contentious cases, it was said, would compromise the political neutrality of the judges. Moreover, the Commission thought there was no demand for a Bill of Rights to limit the powers of the Westminster Parliament, and it would be inconsistent to make a different proposal with regard to the Scottish and Welsh Assemblies. However, there has recently been a revival of enthusiasm for a Bill of Rights, both inside the Conservative Party and in outside circles. It stems largely from the influential lectures of Sir Leslie Scarman [*English Law — the New Dimension* (Stevens, 1974)] and a series of four articles in May 1975 by Lord Hailsham in *The Times*. The issue now promises to be a happy debating ground for Conservative lawyers.

In the past, Conservatives have been no more enthusiastic about a Bill of Rights than they have been about other proposed constitutional reforms. This attitude has partly been attributable to a scepticism about the value of written, high-sounding 'Declarations of Rights', unfortunately associated with such misadventures as the French Revolution, as compared to the worthy English pragmatism of the common law; it has also been influenced by legal doubts about whether a Bill of Rights is compatible with the doctrine of Parliamentary sovereignty, which asserts that Parliament is always able to repeal earlier legislation. Neither of these reasons for scepticism seems particularly justifiable. There is no rational ground for believing that the formulation of fundamental rights and freedoms in a Bill of Rights is a less reliable means of protection against democratic tyranny than the common law. The reason why early European Bills of Rights were so ineffective is that they were adopted by countries which had no tradition or comprehension of political liberty. This is not the case with the United Kingdom.

The second ground of reservation is of much less weight now that Parliamentary sovereignty has been surrendered through accession to the EEC. (Now that the Referendum is over, Conservatives have no excuse for pretending otherwise.) As Sir Leslie Scarman pointed out in his lectures, the doctrine was in any case never as well established as some constitutional lawyers argued. If, as is now virtually certain, judges will be prepared to strike down legislation which is incompatible with Community regulations, it is improbable that there would be much difficulty over the entrenchment of a Bill of Rights — assuming this is desirable on other grounds.

Some Conservatives see a Bill of Rights as a useful, perhaps an indispensable, weapon in the fight against Socialism. It is possible that this argument may be overstated. Admittedly certain provisions in the Community Land Act (at least as originally drafted) might be attacked on the basis of a right that no person may be deprived of liberty or property without a fair hearing, and it is very probable that the application of the closed shop to the press would fall foul of a 'free speech' right. It has often been argued that some of the immigration legislation might have been struck down by a Supreme Court as violating the fundamental equality of all citizens – certainly it would have been invalid in the United States of America, as would the incitement to racial hatred provision in the Race Relations Act. But of course there is nothing particularly Socialist about immigration legislation, nor was there about the dubious Prevention of Terrorism (Temporary Provisions) Act of 1974, conferring extraordinarily wide powers of arrest and detention on the police. Desirable as it would be to have an additional check on Socialist legislation, particularly in the absence of a strong Second Chamber, Conservatives might, I think, be disappointed in the direct political repercussions of a Bill of Rights.

Nevertheless this does not mean that the reform should not be seriously entertained. To take one area of law, it is arguable that the existing restrictions on free speech, particularly those imposed by the laws of contempt and of libel, are too onerous. At this moment it is possible that English contempt law, as decided by the House of Lords in the *Sunday Times* thalidomide case, might be held by the European Court of Human Rights to be in violation of the European Convention for the Protection of Human Rights and Fundamental Freedoms as failing adequately to protect freedom of speech. (In a number of cases in the last two years the English courts have taken notice of this Convention, holding that there is a strong presumption that Parliament does not intend legislation to conflict with it.) Conservatives should welcome the expansion of civil liberties which might in the long term ensue from the judicial development of a Bill of Rights. They should not be too concerned whether it immediately cuts down the ambit of Socialist law-making.

The implications of a Bill of Rights, however, may not be wholly attractive to Conservatives. Freedom of speech, for example, may under a Bill be protected in areas such as obscene publications where some Conservatives have been more inclined to adopt an anti-libertarian stance. It is for this reason that pressure for reform in these areas has more often come from the left in politics. Indeed in February 1976 a Labour Party committee has reported in favour of a Bill of Rights along the lines of the European Convention. Moreover, Professor Oakeshott has warned that freedom of speech and the press are not as valuable safeguards of political liberty as the dispersal of power which results from the opportunity to own private property. [See the essay, 'The Political Economy of Freedom' in *Rationalism in Politics* (Methuen, 1962, reprinted 1974).] Despite these caveats, Conservatives should contemplate the enactment of a Bill of Rights as an additional safeguard against the threat of more authoritarian government and as some protection for individual liberties. In itself it is not perhaps of the first importance, but if there is to be a serious measure of devolution, it would certainly be appropriate to contend for the inclusion of a Bill of Rights in the new constitutional settlement. This has been advocated by Lord Hailsham in the articles referred to. Conservatives should not hesitate to entrench civil liberties against repeal by Act of Parliament, as only then are these fundamental rights immune from challenge by a temporary majority.

All Governments talk constantly about relaxation of the secrecy laws and the need for more open government, and most of them disappoint the expectations aroused. On opening up the *arcana imperii* to the people and on devising new methods of redress for the abuse of power, the Conservatives' record has been dismal. The Macmillan Government only reluctantly accepted the recommendation of the Franks Committee on Tribunals and Inquiries (1958) that inspectors' reports at planning inquiries be published. A few years later the same administration refused to introduce legislation to implement the Justice Committee's proposals for the appointment of an Ombudsman. Finally, the Heath Government, having set up a Department Committee under Lord Franks to investigate the Official Secrets legislation, adopted a lukewarm attitude to the implementation of its recommendations. Naturally, any judgement about a relaxation of secrecy or the institution of new Parliamentary or legal machinery for the review of administrative activity must be arrived at after an assessment of the competing arguments. Too often, however, Conservatives appear to be so influenced by outmoded constitutional doctrine and habitual attitudes that they are precluded from making any sensible judgement. The attempted justification of the refusal to contemplate a Parliamentary Commissioner by resort to the Ministerial Responsibility doctrine is a classic example of this. Conservatives see themselves, perhaps, as still opposed to the Liberals with their supposedly anarchist tendencies, when the real opposition is by its ideology more dirigiste and paternalist than Conservatives should ever want to be.

Not all Conservatives fit into this pattern. T. E. Utley's *Occasion for Ombudsman* [Christopher Johnson, 1961] influenced a number of Conservative backbenchers in their advocacy of the Parliamentary Commissioner. One of the principal themes of Ian Gilmour's *The Body Politic* is the excessive secrecy at all levels of British government. In the debate in June 1973 on the Franks Committee Report on the Official Secrets legislation, one or two Conservatives were highly critical of the Heath Government's reception of the report. There is therefore no reason on the basis of recent history why Conservatives should not feel encouraged to take up a more radical approach to these questions.

Repeal of the Official Secrets legislation will by itself merely reduce the number of possible criminal prosecutions for unauthorised disclosure of official information. But it might reduce the prevailing atmosphere of government secrecy. When the Labour Government's Bill is introduced, the Opposition should ensure that there is some procedure for reviewing a Ministerial classification of information as secret. If the courts are now competent to review claims to Crown privilege (see *Conway* v. *Rimmer*), there seems no good reason why they — or perhaps, alternatively, a committee of the Privy Council — should not have the power finally to decide whether information should be classified for the purposes of the new legislation. Secondly, although the Franks Committee was unenthusiastic about giving citizens a legal right to obtain non-secret government information, equivalent to the rights enjoyed by citizens in Sweden and the United States, it is hoped that the Conservatives will press for the inclusion of such a right in the legislation.

One of the prevalent myths in British politics is that secrecy, of which one aspect is the confidentiality of the relationship between Minister and adviser, necessarily improves the quality of government. The reverse is probably the case. Secrecy is as likely to lead to delay as to expedite vital decisions: keeping the public out of the picture reduces popular pressure and induces a false sense of complacency. The appearance that all Ministers and Departments are in total agreement over every government policy is deceptive; the façade is preserved, supposedly to make government more effective and dignified. In fact, it impoverishes national disccussion of the issues without dispelling public anxiety, and effectively reduces the flexibility of government. At the same time it enhances the influence of those privileged pressure groups who enjoy the confidence of the Government; over their discussions and correspondence is thrown the mantle of secrecy. Some months before the change in counter-inflation policy in the summer of 1975, many Labour Ministers must have had doubts about the viability of the 'social contract', and naturally these would have been expressed to the TUC. The public only had intimations of this. With more information about the Government's doubts, press and popular pressure for a tougher policy would have grown, and this might have strengthened the Government's hand in its negotiations with the trade union movement.

Secrecy also reduces the acceptability of administrative decisions. This is, for example, the case in the fields of welfare administration (for some mysterious reason, the Supplementary Benefits 'A' Code is still not published) and of town and country planning — though it is admittedly less the case in this latter area than it used to be. In a free and democratic society the acceptability of decisions is as important as their 'objective' correctness — indeed, it is impossible to separate the two criteria. Government secrecy insulates the politician from the people, so that it is impossible to disagree with Ian Gilmour's striking conclusion: 'Secrecy thus produces the contrary result of what is intended; fear, not leadership of public opinion' [The Body Politic, p. 17].

Much of this can only be changed through the gradual erosion of outmoded attitudes. But something can be accomplished by institutional reform. The Conservatives should give some thought as to how this might be brought about most effectively. A familiar suggestion is for a strengthening of the Parliamentary Committee system. This is not primarily a matter of increasing the range of policy areas covered by Select Committees. It is rather allowing such committees to cross-examine ministers and civil servants at the stage of policy formation, forcing the administration to disclose the reasoning behind its programme. The Executive would probably gain as much from this exchange as Parliament. Secondly, Departmental Committees of Inquiry should be conducted in public, unless there is a very good reason for a secret session. Thirdly, an advantage of the Industrial Parliament or consultative assembly, at one time favoured by Churchill and taken up by the Conservatives in 1974, would be that consultation with the TUC, CBI and other represented organisations might often be held in public.

The reforms — electoral, constitutional and administrative — discussed in this chapter may not be equally important. They are all, however, worthy of serious consideration in preparing for the next Conservative Government. Doubtless when that time comes other matters, such as the handling of the economy and industrial relations, will present themselves as of much more significance in the short term. But the wise statesman does not believe that a year, let alone a week, is a long time in politics. He (or she) must one day leave the political stage, confident that the constitution and the institutions of the nation are worthy of respect. Nothing less can be demanded of a trustee.

Many people, both at home and abroad, on the right and the moderate left of politics, doubt the ability of democracy and free institutions to survive this century. The tasks governments assume for themselves, or have imposed on them, grow more numerous and become more complex. The tendency is inevitably to standardise and to centralise. At first, the public makes more demands on government, and then it grows restless as these demands are not met, or the attempt leads to intolerable impositions on personal freedom. This road can only lead to civil turmoil or authoritarian rule, and perhaps both.

One way to avert this crisis is for government to encourage people and communities to do more for themselves, to devolve power to the individual. This is why Conservatives encourage parental involvement and choice in education, and voluntary work in welfare. It is also partly why they are beginning to take a serious interest in employee participation in industry. But in the context of our society, which is used to demanding much from government, there may be limits to what can be done by this avenue — at least until the public has recovered fully from the 'collectivist' disease. Another approach, wholly compatible with the first, is constitutionally to limit the powers of government, and to break up monopolies of power within the institutional structure of government. This goal might be accomplished by devolution, separating national and regional government and allocating powers to both. And it would also be achieved by electoral reform, ensuring that no party had a monopoly of power.

The reforms I have been discussing should, therefore, be examined for their utility in preserving for posterity our traditional liberties, as well as in the context of the very practical questions posed in the first paragraph of this essay. The conclusions suggested do entail a thorough reappraisal of many Conservative preconceptions. But for a true Conservative there should be nothing particularly difficult in that!

4 Foreign Policy

C. M. WOODHOUSE

No country today can have a completely independent foreign policy. Perhaps this was always true, but it was not always seen to be true. Hence the innumerable wars to which the system of sovereign states has given rise. But today there is the difference that no state, however powerful, really believes (though some still pretend to believe it) that it can exercise and enforce its will regardless of others. Minor powers of course always had to recognise this fact, though paradoxically some minor powers nowadays, like Uganda under President Amin, can literally get away with murder. Major powers, on the other hand, have only recently learned the lesson: the French and British Governments in the Middle East in 1956, the Soviet Government in the Cuba crisis of 1962, the US Government in Vietnam between 1965 and 1975.

It may seem optimistic to believe that the Chinese Communist Government, or even the Soviet Government, has really learned this lesson. Although Khrushchev recognised the constraints on his independence when confronted by real strength and determination on the part of the USA, it appears that Brezhnev has been bolder and more successful in using the threat of massive armaments overseas, particularly in Angola and other areas of ex-colonial Africa. But his successes were chiefly due to American weakness and irresolution in the aftermath of Vietnam and the Watergate scandal. The failure of nerve in the United States should prove to be no more characteristic or permanent than 'appeasement' was in Britain. So even today the Soviet Government would find it exceedingly dangerous to ignore the lesson that there can be no completely independent foreign policy. Whether the Chinese Communists have also learned the lesson is admittedly less certain, but they at least appear to respect it in practice. Fortunately dictators nowadays, unlike Hitler and Stalin, behave more rationally than they talk.

Given, then, that total independence in foreign policy no longer exists, the problem of the sovereign state today is to assess correctly the nature of its interests and its capacity to secure them. Britain's interests, like those of other industrialised Western powers, are easy to define: international peace and justice, freedom under the rule of law, and economic prosperity. They are interconnected and indivisible. That is to say, none of them can be achieved unless they are all achieved. It follows that, since we cannot enforce a worldwide *Pax Britannica*, we must support international arrangements to achieve the same end.

The British are traditionally suspicious of international arrangements, which they refer to often as 'foreign entanglements'. It makes no difference whether they are peacetime alliances like NATO or permanent institutions like the United Nations. There is some reason for mistrust. Of our present alliances, CENTO and SEATO inspire little confidence; and at least one-third of the signatories of the North Atlantic Treaty are a good deal less than wholehearted members of the alliance.

It requires an effort of memory to recall that CENTO (once the Baghdad Pact, until Iraq defected from it) and SEATO (formed in the aftermath of the French defeat in Indo-China) are still in existence, but on paper they are. The North Atlantic Treaty is slightly less of a scrap of paper. But it never corresponded to strategic necessity in confrontation with the Soviet bloc, since it could not include the key territories of Sweden, Switzerland, Austria, Ireland or Spain. Today its utility is further circumscribed: France and Greece have actually withdrawn from the military command structure; Turkey's co-operation has been prejudiced by the Cyprus dispute, Iceland's by the 'cod war', Italy's and Portugal's by internal problems; Norway and Denmark would allow no foreign units on their soil; Canada talks of reducing her contribution, and so does even the USA from time to time. Britain's own record towards NATO under the Wilson Government only made things worse. It could be justified only on the extreme assumption that the alliance was already virtually useless anyway.

The United Nations has also been regarded with marked distrust in Britain, along with other international organisations. In contrast with NATO, it is on the Conservative rather than the Labour side that the distrust has been strongest, though the example was set by Ernest Bevin, Foreign Secretary in the first post-war Labour Government. It is true that our experience of the UN and its agencies has not been happy, though I shall argue that this is partly our own fault. But wherever the fault may lie, it is certain that the only remedy for institutions which prove inadequate is to reform and strengthen them. If the UN did not exist, there would be an irresistible demand for the creation of such an institution. So there can be no question of Britain abandoning the UN, though equally none of treating it uncritically. Apart from any question of obligation, this is in our own interests, as I have defined them, every one of which is specified in the preamble to the UN Charter.

The reason why the British tend to mistrust international institutions is that many of us fail to understand what they actually are. They are supplementary mechanisms for adjusting international relations, with certain collective powers which vary from case to case, but are in every case strictly limited. But the British sometimes see them as super-governments with overriding powers, operated entirely by foreigners. This delusion is to be found at both ends of the political spectrum. Left-wing and liberal opinion sometimes wants the UN to be regarded as a super-government — for instance, over the Suez crisis or Rhodesia — and quite mistakenly accuses Conservative Governments of 'flouting' the UN. Right-wing opinion regards it as dangerous even to belong to organisations like the UN or the EEC, for fear of being 'bossed about' by meddling foreigners. Both make the mistake of failing to assess accurately our capacity for securing our national interests within the new international system. Compared to other powers of similar capacity, such as France, West Germany or Japan, we have shown a marked propensity to miscalculate our capacity, chiefly because we have scorned to calculate at all. We have allowed instinct and habit to prevail over reason.

The most striking example of this defect was the long hesitation before we joined the EEC, compounded by the scarcely less damaging hesitation of the Labour Paty even after we had joined. But there have been other examples, which do more credit to our hearts than our heads. We have loyally but quixotically supported allies who were doomed to succumb, such as the royal dynasties of Iraq and Greece, or the Portuguese in Africa and the Americans in South-East Asia. We have been associated in Africa, Asia, the Middle East, and even in Europe, with outmoded régimes or doomed enterprises. British policy has shown the same qualities of loyalty, tenacity and justice as in the days of imperialism, but without the Empire and often towards lost causes. We have preserved the paternalism of an imperial power without the power. A kind of sentimental fallacy has lain at the root of policy-making.

Nowhere has the fallacy taken more absurd forms than in the context of the Commonwealth. An emotional public opinion has impelled successive Governments to subordinate national interest, and even reason and justice, for far too long to the interests of others because they 'stood by us' in the Second World War. Thus, because the European Economic Community was expected to damage Australian and New Zealand trade, and because Australia and New Zealand had stood by us in the war, we were expected to refuse to join the EEC; and because white Rhodesians had stood by us in the war, we were expected to tolerate the African policies of the Smith Government. This kind of argument is not only ludicrous in itself: it is also applied with selective hypocrisy. No one who uses it, for example, has ever argued that we should back the Greeks against the Turks in Cyprus on the ground that Greece 'stood by us' in the war while Turkey remained neutral.

Different varieties of the sentimental fallacy have infected both of the major political parties. The Conservative Party has retained the sense of a superior wisdom to other countries in foreign affairs, the Labour Party has retained the sense of unlimited moral obligations. By relying on instinct and habit rather than hard-headed reasoning, we have frequently failed to estimate correctly our capacity for action. Usually we have overestimated it, as in the Suez crisis of 1956 and the Rhodesia crisis of 1965. Occasionally we have underestimated it, as in the Cyprus crisis of 1974. Almost always we have failed to take account of the extra leverage to be gained by international support through the United Nations.

It is fair to mention the occasional exceptions. It was right, but not easy, for the Conservative Government in 1954 to refuse to be drawn by the United States into a war in Indo-China alongside the French. It was right, but not easy, for the Labour Government in 1968 to refuse to support the secession of Biafra from the Nigerian Federation. It was right, but not easy, for both parties in succession to persevere in the effort to establish full diplomatic relations with the Chinese Communist Government, even at the expense of a sharp breach with US policy. These were all cases in which an accurate assessment was made of our national interests and of our capacity to achieve them, alone or in partnership.

Capacity for effective action is a necessary but invidious concept in international relations. It is a function of physical, material and economic strength. In saying this I do not mean to belittle the power of moral influence and rational persuasion. On the contrary, where individual strength is insufficient (which in our case it virtually always is), it is a function of these as well. But moral influence and rational persuasion are only alternative and better ways of using material strength, not substitutes for it. If one does not have the strength in the first place, they are valueless, as the League of Nations found to our cost. It is to the bases of strength, then, that we must first look in formulating foreign policy. International politics and diplomacy are merely the application of them.

Strength lies in economic, technological and military factors. By any measurement of any of them, Britain cannot stand alone in the world. We are increasingly dependent on foreign capital. We rely on imported raw materials and food to a greater extent than any other industrialised nation. We cannot sustain, from our own national resources, the overheads of major projects in the field of advanced technology; nor have we, in our own islands, a sufficient market for them. Our small islands are over-populated and virtually indefensible in modern warfare. All these considerations oblige us to enter into international arrangements, though these vary in different contexts. Examples are: borrowing from OPEC countries; joining the EEC; supporting NATO and other alliances. These are the necessary protection of our long-term interests.

They do not mean that we have no capacity to act effectively as a nation in a crisis. They mean only that effective action must be action in concert, and the possibility of obtaining support and acquiescence in a crisis depends on careful nurture of our relations when there is no crisis. A striking example of a crisis which impinged on all industrialised and developing countries alike, especially our own, was the Arab-Israeli war of October 1973, followed by the oil crisis (and compounded, in our own case, by a coalminers' strike). The West was in a weak position economically because the oil-producing countries of the Middle East had a strong grip on our fuel supplies. Among them, not only were the Arabs bitterly hostile to Israel, but Iran simultaneously decided to exploit the crisis by quadrupling the price of oil. To be fair, the Shah's decision was motivated not so much by hostility to Israel (which is little felt in Iran) as by the need to offset the effects of Western inflation on industrial imports into his country. The result in any case was that in economic terms the Western powers had a capacity to put pressure only on Israel, not on the Arabs.

In military terms, however, the balance was more even. Since all the Middle Eastern belligerents were dependent on weapons supplied by the great powers, and since the great powers were determined not to be drawn into armed conflict with each other, some degree of control could be exercised by international 'crisis management'. This was mainly the work of the US and Soviet Governments, but the British and French played an ancillary part, which neither of them could have played alone. Such combinations must in future become the normal pattern of foreign policy. They may be semi-permanent institutions, like NATO or the EEC; they may be loose and informal, like the Commonwealth; or they may be occasional, to meet sudden emergencies. In the last case, the most suitable mechanism for creating *ad hoc* combinations is, in principle, the United Nations, but only provided that the mechanism is kept in good working order.

What would good working order be? It can best be illustrated by reference to the missed opportunities. There have been many, but the most glaring was the failure ever to refer Vietnam to the UN. It could be argued that this was not Britain's business, though that would be a feeble argument for a power occupying one of the permanent seats in the Security Council. In any case it was not Harold Wilson's view in 1965, as he showed by his ridiculous attempt at a 'Commonwealth initiative', followed by the even more ridiculous despatch of a Parliamentary Under-Secretary to put things right. It is said that he dared not offend the United States by raising the matter in the Security Council because he needed US support for sterling; but a better solution to that problem would have been for Britain to live within her means. If Vietnam had been referred to the UN in 1965, as it should have been, then there would have been no difficulty about bringing the crises in the Lebanon and Angola before the UN ten years later. It may be that the UN could not have done much, but that is no excuse for not allowing it to do anything.

It is customary to blame the imperfections of the UN on the irresponsible conduct of the newer members, as exemplified in the anti-Zionist resolutions in 1975. It would be fairer to blame it on the failure of the original members to establish proper conventions and codes of conduct before the newer members joined. In this respect the contrast between the UN and the Commonwealth is very marked. But it is never too late to mend. For no country is it more important than for Britain that the mechanisms of the UN should be repaired, since there is such an enormous disproportion between the scale of our interests abroad and our capacity for independent action. We should, therefore, see the UN as a valuable adjunct to foreign policy, not as an interfering nuisance to be kept at bay. We could, for example, have used its services with advantage in both of our most intractable current problems, those of Rhodesia and Northern Ireland; but only if we had placed our trust in the UN during the previous twenty years, and thereby earned its trust when we needed it. This is not a matter of starry-eyed idealism, but of practical expediency. The obstacle to such a line of policy was the concept of national sovereignty, and in particular the rule debarring the UN from intervening in matters of 'domestic jurisdiction'. But in practice we had already recognised the obsolescence of these notions in the case of Cyprus, and Harold Macmillan had provided a philosophic justification for doing so in his speech in 1960 on the 'Wind of Change' in southern Africa.

The dilution of sovereignty was again an issue in the debate on Britain's entry into the EEC. It alarmed both the right and the left, though for different reasons. The right argued in terms of old-fashioned nationalism, almost of imperialism, making much of the supposed betrayal of the Commonwealth. The left feared that membership of the EEC would inhibit progress towards total Socialism. As a matter of fact, the fears of the left were to some extent justified: witness the rules of competition imposed by the EEC on the British Steel Corporation, which gave much satisfaction to the small surviving private sector of the steel industry in Britain. Many Conservatives strangely failed to see that this principle of ideology was the real objection of Socialists to the EEC. They thus allowed themselves to be misled by sterile arguments about sovereignty, and entirely misconceived arguments about loyalty to the Commonwealth.

It is, of course, true that a measure of sovereignty, in the sense of an entirely independent power of decision, was given up in signing the Treaty of Rome. If it had not been, there would have been no point in the Treaty. Considering that most of the wars of the last five hundred years have been the consequence of national sovereignty, it should hardly be a matter of regret. But a great deal of casuistry was devoted to explaining it away. It was often pointed out, for example, that the British Parliament could still, in the last resort, prevent the Council of Ministers in Brussels from adopting legislation of which we disapproved. It was less often pointed out that our Parliament would no longer have the undivided power subsequently to amend or repeal such legislation. It would have been more to the point to have explained that this was part of the trend of the times, which had already been accepted with much less demur a quarter of a century earlier in signing the North Atlantic Treaty. Membership of NATO obliges us to give up absolute control over issues of peace and war, since it requires us to treat an attack on any other member as an attack on ourselves. It even goes beyond our commitment to the EEC, because the power to force a war upon us actually lies outside the membership of NATO, whereas in the EEC our power of decision is surrendered only to a collective body of which we are ourselves members with a technical right of veto.

Those who really suffer from ideological anxieties about sovereignty can comfort themselves with the thought that there is no such thing as a treaty which cannot be denounced, and that so long as the House of Commons exists it can repeal the European Communities Act, if it so wishes. If this were not so, the referendum in 1975 would have been total fraud. But these were not the real considerations in the minds of Conservative objectors to the Treaty of Rome. They were animated rather, as Conservative foreign policy too often has been, by sentiment, instinct and habit. Hence the impassioned arguments about loyalty to the Commonwealth.

It was only in the closing stages of the great debate that the Commonwealth Governments almost unanimously admitted, what in fact had been obvious for many years, that they stood to gain substantially from Britain's membership of the EEC. Most of them had seen the implications of the changing pattern of world trade well before Britain's first application to join the Community in 1961, and had made their dispositions accordingly. Our application was a belated reaction to changes which were already well advanced among the developed countries of the Commonwealth. The developing countries soon learned the same lesson. During the years when we were excluded from the EEC, a number of them made trade agreements with the EEC on their own account. All of them want to trade with the prosperous countries of Western Europe as well as with Britain. If we were outside the EEC, they would by-pass Britain and make their own arrangements. The ties of the Commonwealth would thus have grown weaker. Now that we are inside the EEC, they have a familiar and sympathetic point of contact in Brussels, and the ties of the Commonwealth will grow stronger. Our choice, in fact, was never between the Commonwealth and the Common Market, but between having both and having neither.

The debate over Britain's entry into the EEC would have proved much less troublesome if it had been seen from the first that there was no real conflict between Britain's national interest and the wider international and Commonwealth interest. One of the unfortunate legacies of paternalist imperialism is that we must always put our own interests last. From this flows the tacit *non sequitur* that what appears to be in our own interest must be contrary to the interests of other more deserving peoples, and must, therefore, be rejected. Socialists happily exploit this liberal humbug, to which Conservatives too readily succumb. The truth is that our national interests, rationally considered, rarely conflict with wider international interests, and still more rarely with our moral obligations. On the contrary, experience shows that we are more likely to harm our national interests when we fail to take the course which is morally right.

The classic illustration of this principle was and always will be the appeasement of Nazi Germany. Fortunately the lesson was learned to some extent. There has been less inclination to appease Soviet Russia, though under Harold Wilson one cannot say there has been none. But there are other cases which illustrate the same principle — for instance, southern Africa under the white nationalist governments, and Greece under the military dictatorship of 1967–74. In both cases British Governments subordinated moral considerations to a supposed national interest: defence or trade or both. In both cases they were wrong on pragmatic as well as moral grounds.

In Africa it should have been clear long since that trade with the black states would become vastly more important than with the whites. The defence interest has also proved illusory, and this seems to have been long recognised by the Chiefs of Staff; for even in 1971, under a Conservative Government, the map of our worldwide defence commitments in the Defence White Paper contrived to omit South Africa altogether. As for Greece, the prolonged toleration of the military dictatorship by the British and American Governments contributed disastrously to the Cyprus crisis of 1974, which caused both Greece and Turkey to substantially abandon their commitments to NATO. In each case the (pragmatically) right course would have been the course which was (morally) right. The traditional doctrine that we had no right to intervene in the internal affairs of independent countries became tantamount in practice to intervention on the side of a tyrannical *status quo*. Even if active intervention is inadmissible, it is short-sighted to appear to confer approval on tyrannies by alliances, ministerial visits, summit meetings, arms supplies and diplomatic recognition.

These cases help to clarify two fallacies about foreign policy which derive from traditional habits of thought. One is that there is a watertight distinction between the external relations of sovereign states, which are the proper field of international concern, and their internal affairs, which are not. There are in fact innumerable transnational links in the modern world to which that old-fashioned distinction no longer applies. International relations in the strict sense form only one of many webs or 'systems' which stretch across the surface of the globe, though still an important one. Others are strategic, industrial, financial, intellectual, ideological, religious, and so on. Multinational companies, Communist parties, Christian churches and Islam, Zionism, Women's Lib, Pop Culture, revolutionary anarchism, and so on, are other examples. No government can by its own undivided efforts control all their operations, and many do not want to do so.

Secondly, it is a fallacious assumption that moral considerations and national interest are distinct and commonly in conflict. This fallacy is one to which the British people, still cherishing some of the habits of an imperial power, seem to be peculiarly prone. Those who still believe in 'my country right or wrong' think that it does not matter putting national interest above moral considerations. Those who take a more high-minded view think we have an absolute obligation to subordinate our national interest to moral considerations, which generally means to someone else's national interest. What neither sufficiently realise is that in the overwhelming majority of cases our duty and our interest are one and the same. This is not to say that dilemmas never arise in foreign policy: they do, but they are of a different kind. A frequent example is the dilemma between justice and peace – both absolute requirements defined in the preamble to the UN Charter, but sometimes irreconcilable. Sometimes we and our allies have felt compelled to sacrifice justice in order to maintain peace, as in the Hungarian crisis of 1956 and the Czechoslovak crisis of 1968. Sometimes we have upheld justice at the expense of peace, as in Korea in the 1950s. Such dilemmas are unavoidable, but they do not pose a conflict between moral obligation and national interest, only between two moral obligations.

The same dilemma arose, and was much more controversially resolved, in other cases: for example, over the Anglo-French intervention against Egypt in 1956, and the American intervention in Vietnam. For my part, in consistency with my general theme, I should argue that what went wrong in both cases was not a moral judgement, but a pragmatic one. The errant governments thought that they could do what was in fact beyond their unaided powers. The lesson was once more that no power – not even a superpower – can conduct a completely independent foreign policy in 'splendid isolation'. Like every other country, a superpower needs to form combinations and seek a consensus, or at least international acquiescence, before it takes drastic action. Had the British and French Governments tried to do so in 1956, or the US Government in 1965, they would never have launched their fateful ventures, for they would have found that no consensus was to be had.

The consequences of these traumatic shocks are still with us. The worst shock for the French and British Governments was to find themselves let down, as they saw it, by the Americans; the worst shock for the Americans was to find themselves let down by the British. The French recovered fairly quickly, because political opinion in France was not divided over the Suez Canal crisis as it was in Britain. The direct consequences were the French decision to establish an independent nuclear deterrent, the return to power of de Gaulle, and the withdrawal of French forces from NATO. No such speedy recovery was available to the British. The question was, and still is, whether anything worth calling a 'special relationship' with the USA could ever be restored. The experience of Vietnam a decade later seemed to suggest that it could not. But this may turn out to be a false conclusion. The growing inequality of wealth and power is not necessarily a decisive factor, for the special relationship never did rest on material equality, which was already vanishing before it began.

Until the Middle East crisis of 1956, American statesmen and officials had a particular respect for British judgement in foreign policy. They would co-operate more readily and more closely with British colleagues than with those of any other nationality, especially in the Middle East. Such co-operation, for example, led to the overthrow of Musaddiq in Iran (the nationalist leader who expropriated the British-owned oil industry) and the resolution of the Anglo-Iranian oil crisis in 1953. It was probably the last such operation by the British authorities, and the first by the Americans. Nothing like it has been repeated on a joint basis. But even after 1956 there was still a willingness on the American side to revive the 'special relationship'. Under President Kennedy and Harold Macmillan there was in fact a brief revival. The Cuba crisis in 1962 was managed practically as a joint Anglo-American operation, as Macmillan's memoirs show; and the initiative for it came from Kennedy. Later still, President Johnson hoped to revive it again, but he found Harold Wilson too untrustworthy, especially over Vietnam.

Although it is customary to argue that the changed roles of Britain and the USA absolutely preclude any further revival of the 'special relationship', I am not sure that this is necessarily true. A lingering respect for Britain still survives in the United States. Now that we have decided to stay in the EEC, there is likely to be a considerable increase of investment by American industry in the United Kingdom, as the best route of entry into the Common Market. The relationship will continue to be unequal, but less so psychologically than materially. The events of the last ten years have reduced the Americans' consciousness of power and self-confidence in their international, almost imperialist role. A community of deflating and even humiliating experience has perhaps put Britain and USA more nearly on all fours than twenty years ago. This could be a major asset for British foreign policy. It even justifies de Gaulle's fear that Britain in the EEC would prove to be a Trojan Horse for the USA.

It does not point, however, either in Europe or in the wider world, to the kind of dual hegemony which prevailed in the Second World War on the Western side. It is merely one new balancing factor in the new concert of nations. The old polarisation of power has disappeared for good, along with the undivided sovereignty of the nation-state. Indeed, the very evolution of events which inflicted the common experience of humiliation on the British and American Governments over the last twenty years has also shown the vastly increased power of small states and even non-states (such as the Palestinian Liberation Organisation or the Irish Republican Army) to force their will upon the international community. It is no longer tenable to argue that one will never negotiate or come to terms with those who resort to lawlessness, revolution or violence in pursuit of national or ideological aims. One may have to do so. Just because the established powers are determined not to be dragged into another general war, the way is open to lesser powers and pressure groups to pursue their aims by force, as never before. There is already a long list of revolutionary leaders with whom different Western powers − British, French, Belgian, Dutch, Spanish, Portuguese − said they would never negotiate, and whom we now recognise as heads of state. There is an equally long list of cases of territorial aggression which succeeded because the price of resistance was too high: for example, among the lesser powers alone, by the Indians in Goa, the Israelis in Sinai, the Iranians in the Persian Gulf, the Turks in Cyprus, the North Vietnamese in South Vietnam, and the Cubans in Angola.

If there is to be any remedy for this upsurge of violence in international relations, it clearly cannot lie in unilateral action by any power, least of all Britain. It must rest on concerted action, which can only be procured through an international organisation. The most obvious examples of this principle, though not the most important, are the hijacking of aircraft and the kidnapping of diplomatists. A much wider range of violent activities, from open warfare to urban guerrillas, can also only be confronted on the basis of international consensus. This is not to say that individual governments have no power of separate action and no right to undertake it. On the contrary, in certain cases they have an obligation to do so, but only where both an international and an internal consensus will support them. Both kinds of consensus were lacking when the British Government acted in the Suez Canal crisis of 1956. It may be asked, then, in what circumstances would such action be justified?

A case worth examining, because it illustrates all the principles adumbrated in this paper, is that of Cyprus. Britain's rights and obligations in Cyprus go back nearly a century, but it will suffice to consider them over the last thirty years. Before 1960, they rested on the island's colonial status, since 1960 on a Treaty of Guarantee. Practically throughout, British policy has been haphazard and indecisive, reacting to events and always falling behind them. When the crisis of 1974 hit the island, with the attempt by Greek army officers to overthrow President Makarios, the British Government did nothing whatever. Yet Cyprus was one of the few places in the world in which Britain had an absolutely clear and specific responsibility, and would have received universal support in upholding it. Whatever was the right thing for Britain to do in July 1974, it cannot have been nothing whatever.

The chronicle of failure in dealing with Cyprus over thirty years amply confirms the diagnosis that British foreign policy has rested on habit, instinct and sentiment rather than foresight and reasoning. The original mistake lay in failing to see Cyprus as a problem in foreign policy at all. It was seen first as a colonial problem and secondly as an aspect of defence. Thus, when the Foreign Office was prepared in 1945 to concede the island's union with Greece (*Enosis*), it was overruled by objections from the Colonial Office and the Chiefs of Staff. If later events had been more accurately foreseen at the time, it would have been clear that *Enosis* in 1945 would have been the least unsatisfactory solution of the problem. At that date the Turkish Government had neither the legal right, nor the moral standing, nor even the inclination to oppose it. The general trend of future events was not in fact unforeseeable, for some of the Labour Government's advisers foresaw it. The decision taken to do nothing cannot even be called a miscalculation for there was no calculation at all; and so it continued for another generation.

When outbreaks of violence twice forced reconsideration of the problem (between 1954 and 1960, and again in 1974), two more totally impracticable solutions were brought forward: an independent republic based on 'power-sharing' between the Greeks and Turks; and a federal or confederal state based on 'cantons'. No attention was paid to the fact that both are extremely sophisticated systems, likely to succeed only among people predisposed to live in harmony. 'Power-sharing' broke down even in the Lebanon, let alone Northern Ireland: it had no more hope in Cyprus than in pre-partition Palestine. Federation broke down in every one of the ex-British possessions where it was tried; and even in the most mature states it has come under strain. In the case of Cyprus these expedients were mere evasions of the problem, in the hope that it would go away. Only after the crisis of July 1974 did rational thought begin to be applied to it for the first time.

The failure of the Labour Government to do anything in fulfilment of the Treaty of Guarantee left a situation in which no political solution was possible apart from the economically disastrous expedient of partition. Partition can be either open — for example, by double *Enosis*, which means the annexation of the two parts of the island to Greece and Turkey respectively — or disguised, for example in a federal or cantonal system. During 1975 it became clear that the British Government was becoming committed to one or other of these expedients. This was the implication of the decision to allow Turkish refugees in the British bases in southern (Greek-held) Cyprus to leave for the Turkish mainland, in the certain knowledge that they would be re-settled in the northern (Turkish-held) part of the island. Such a deliberately contrived shift of populations could have only one meaning and only one outcome, which cannot have escaped the British Government. It therefore ranks as the first calculated act of policy by any British Government since Cyprus became a Crown Colony. But it was perhaps not a very good calculation.

Without prejudice to the question whether any particular calculation was right or wrong, wise or unwise, it is my contention that foreign policy should be based on calculation rather than alternating bouts of inertia and impulse. British foreign policy since the Second World War has been generally in conflict with this principle. Not many episodes show the marks of calculation in any notable degree. Calculation means basically making an accurate assessment of the nation's capacity, alone or in partnership, to influence and determine events. This hardly seemed necessary when Britain's power was very great, and was even thought (quite mistakenly) to be absolute. But old habits die hard, and recently, when it has become increasingly necessary, we have not been very good calculators. The case of Cyprus, where there could be no question of our rights and powers, shows how British Governments first overestimated their command over circumstances (up to 1960) and then abjectly decided that they were totally powerless (in 1974). Similarly in South-East Asia the Labour Government of 1964 first overestimated its powers (in the 'East of Suez' policy, which led to Harold Wilson's interventions in Vietnam) and then abjectly scuttled from the area altogether. These do not even deserve to be called miscalculations: they were non-calculations.

Rather surprisingly, since the Conservative Party has the reputation of being non-doctrinaire, Conservative Foreign Secretaries have shown more disposition towards calculation. Eden and Macmillan were both calculators, though both made mistakes: Eden in dealing with Dulles and Nasser, Macmillan in dealing with de Gaulle. But in the long run miscalculations do less harm than crude hunches. Labour Foreign Secretaries have tended to be tough, 'no-nonsense' men like Ernest Bevin, Herbert Morrison, George Brown and James Callaghan, who identify other people's susceptibilities with nonsense. They seldom learn from their mistakes because they are unaware of having made any. There are, of course, exceptions to these generalisations on both sides — Selwyn Lloyd on the one and Michael Stewart on the other; but these two were both completely dominated by their Prime Ministers. What is certain is that we shall need calculating rather than instinctive men at the Foreign and Commonwealth Office for the rest of the century.

The most important calculation to be made will be the exact assessment of Britain's residual power. It will be difficult, because the answer will vary at different periods and in different circumstances. It will be equally a mistake to overestimate it, as was done up to about 1960, and to underestimate it, as was done in the decade after 1965. The most difficult part of the calculation will be the extent to which the diminution of our individual power as a nation can be counterbalanced by alliances and other associations. Considering all the instruments of leverage available to us, my personal judgement is that no value at all is to be expected from summit conferences such as Helsinki; very little from either military alliances or the Commonwealth; rather more from the 'special relationship' with the USA; and most of all from international institutions, especially the United Nations, if we apply ourselves to using them effectively. The last qualification is all-important. It is no longer a matter of idealistic lip-service, but of supreme national interest.

My conclusion is twofold. Firstly, for a power of the character and relative strength of Britain, the United Nations is without exception the most crucial instrument of foreign policy. It can be generalised in the principle that a country has need of the United Nations in inverse proportion to the balance between its own capacity for effective action and its commitments. Secondly, we have to face the problem that the UN has proved in practice a clumsy and imperfect mechanism. It does not matter where the blame for this fact lies, though it is fair to admit that some of it lies with ourselves. What is certain is that there is no merit in the extremist argument often heard in Britain, France, South Africa and the USA, among other countries, that we should resign from the UN, or ignore it, or liquidate it. Any such course would be in contradiction with my first proposition. The only practical course is to improve and strengthen the mechanism; and there is no way to do this except by our own example. It is strange that this should not be found self-evident by the nation which Pitt once declared 'has saved herself by her exertions, and will, I trust, save Europe by her example'. All that is necessary is to substitute the world for Europe. My final proposition, then, is that we should conduct ourselves at the UN as if it were the sort of organisation we believe it ought to be. There is no other example we can set, and no other course we can follow.

5 The Economic Roles of the State

PETER SINCLAIR

The economy of every country is a kaleidoscope. Some industries expand; others contract. Consumers face changes in income and prices, and alter their pattern of spending. Producers alter their purchases of inputs and their pattern of outputs. In aggregate, there are alternating phases of boom and slump. In the wage hierarchy, we see changes in the positions of different groups; there are also major shifts in the way the nation's income is split into wages, profits and rent. Inflation quickens and slows; and the relative prices of goods are liable to vary, sometimes violently. For most of the relevant variables, trends and fluctuations are hard to distinguish. Against this mercurial backcloth, no change has been more far-reaching, more conspicuous and more controversial than the great expansion in recent decades of the economic role of the Government. 'In the last three years public expenditure has grown by nearly 20 per cent in volume, while output has risen by less than 2 per cent. The ratio of public expenditure to gross domestic product has risen from 50 per cent to 60 per cent. Fifteen years ago it was 42 per cent.' [The quotation comes from the February 1976 Public Expenditure White Paper, Cmnd 6394.] The comparable figure half a century before that – 1910 – was less than 13 per cent. All these percentages (50, 60, 42, 13) are some one-third to two-fifths lower if Government transfers and subsidies to the private sector are subtracted – as they really should be – but the trend is no less marked. Similar, if often less pronounced, changes have occurred in the other Western democracies.

The huge growth in the proportion of national output spent by the Government is only one facet of its increasing economic role. Its spending has been matched – except at times of major fiscal crisis, such as the two World Wars and the period 1973–6 – by parallel increases in the proportion of national income withdrawn in taxes. Since the end of 1972, all medium-sized and large firms have been subject to thorough price controls: increases in prices for the domestic market are subject to strict upper limits enforced by a Government Commission. Perhaps a million workers are likely to see their firms fall under public ownership in the three years 1974–7. There are countless other examples.

It is to the analysis and appraisal of many of the economic roles of government that this chapter is devoted. It will be seen that the errors of the past have lain less in the *principle* of government intervention than in the manner of its *execution*.

The foremost economic activity of governments is the provision of public goods; it is here that the case for government intervention is unassailable. After examining this, we shall turn our attention to the other functions and types of spending that contemporary British government undertakes. The problem of public goods is well illustrated by the parable of the Prisoners' Dilemma.

Two prisoners, in separate cells, are accused of a crime. Each is visited by the prosecutor, who is anxious to secure convictions. 'If you both confess', the prosecutor tells the prisoners separately, 'you will both be sentenced to two years. If you both plead not guilty, you will both be acquitted. But if you confess, and your fellow-prisoner does not, you will only receive a light sentence – one year – while your fellow-prisoner will get five years. Similarly if you plead not guilty and he confesses, you will be sentenced to five years in prison, and he only to one year. I am saying to your fellow-prisoner exactly what I have told you; and of course you know that you plead separately, and that whichever of you is second to plead will not know until later how the other has pleaded.'

What do the two prisoners decide? Both will recognise that the best outcome is for both of them to plead not guilty. But if one says this, while the second confesses, the former will receive a five-year sentence. Each will perceive that the other is likely to play safe and confess; and if there is a serious chance of this, a plea of not guilty is a very unattractive option. We can expect both, therefore, to plead guilty.

Similar dilemmas occur frequently in economic affairs. Their defining characteristic is a divergence between the outcome of individuals' separate attempts to 'optimise' (or choose as best they can), and the outcome of group optimisation. Singly, the prisoners may well opt to plead guilty, thus ensuring that they escape the worst – the five-year sentence; together, the prisoners would surely agree to protest their innocence. Perhaps the clearest parallel in economics is the phenomenon of the public good.

A public good differs from the normal private good in two respects. It can be consumed by everyone; and it cannot be appropriated by anyone. Food and clothing are private goods: the food and clothing consumed by one person cannot be consumed, or used, by someone else; and their 'owner' can usually prevent others from consuming or using them, if he wishes. Under rather strict conditions, it is known that a large number of self-centred individuals, interested only in the satisfaction they desire from private goods, will so arrange their pattern of purchases and sales that it will be impossible to improve the lot of any one of them without loss to at least one other. This result was first demonstrated two centuries ago by

Adam Smith. Much contemporary work in economics is devoted to refining the conditions under which the result holds, and seeing what happens when the conditions fail. The result itself is used widely to justify the doctrine of *laissez-faire* — the view that the automatic working of the free market system produces an allocation of goods to people as good as or better than any other allocation, and that the State should exert as little influence on it as possible.

If there are public goods, on the other hand, this sort of economic anarchy will be inefficient. Individual decision-taking will result in an allocation which is sub-optimal for society: everyone in society could, at least in principle, be made happier by State intervention. The reason is this. An egocentric individual will so try to arrange his purchases that the satisfaction he expects to derive from the last penny spent is the same on every good he consumes. When deciding how much to spend on the provision of a public good, he will ignore the gain that will accrue to others; and he will realise that he can consume what others provide. A society composed of individuals unconcerned with the welfare of others, and attempting to do as well as they can for themselves, will devote too many resources to the production of private goods, and not enough to public goods.

The existence of public goods is beyond doubt. Examples include defence, collective security, the legal system, expenditure to contain contagious disease, and information. The benefit I receive from the provision of defence in no way prevents anyone else deriving benefit; but the beefsteak I eat cannot be consumed by others. I cannot appropriate to myself these benefits from defence. But if the Government were to rely on voluntary contributions to pay for the Royal Navy, I should be tempted to contribute nothing: how much I shall be able to consume in the form of defence services for the Royal Navy will depend immensely more on the contribution of others than on what I contribute; and anything I contribute must be at the expense of the private goods I forgo as a result. The provision of police to deter and detect crime, and courts to assess guilt or innocence and impose penalties, resemble defence in that the satisfaction one person derives from them is in no sense at the expense of the opportunity others have to derive satisfaction too. Contagious disease is a public bad; methods of limiting it (hospitals, inoculation, sewers, rubbish collection) constitute public goods. Information is often difficult to appropriate (a secret has been defined as a statement told to no more than one person at a time); and in some circumstances a piece of knowledge can provide benefit to all. One might think of a natural selection process, working continuously since prehistoric times to eliminate societies which could not resolve the 'prisoners' dilemma' posed by public goods. Correct decisions about public goods require collective organisation and imply some degree of coercion on individuals. Their provision is not costless and must be paid for; voluntary contributions were, as we saw, likely to be grossly insufficient.

Yet 'correct' decisions about public goods are exceedingly problematical. Under ideal conditions, any good is provided optimally when society derives the maximum net advantage from it: marginal benefit will then just equal marginal cost. If everyone is deemed to act in his own interest, if there are no external effects (harmful or favourable) from the consumption or production of any good, and if every buyer and seller acts in perfect markets where there is a unique price for each good at which they can do business, price will measure both marginal benefit and marginal cost; and the market will generate 'correct' levels of production and consumption of everything. But this will not work for public goods, because of their external effects. Assessing the marginal benefit to society from a public good means estimating what everyone would pay if there were a market of the private good type, and adding up the answers. But the problem arises in the first place simply because no such market exists. To make matters worse, the benefits of public goods are conjectural — usually a form of insurance against a social hazard like disease or defeat in war; but there is no objective method of pricing such a catastrophe, and no obvious way of quantifying the risks or the effects of public goods expenditure on them. Furthermore, individuals lack knowledge of relevant details — about military technology or medical research for instance — so that attempts to estimate social benefit from individuals' estimates of value may have little to commend them. Defence raises further difficulties: its value to one country will depend chiefly on its deterrent effect on others; but at the international level, it serves as a macabre instance of the prisoners' dilemma. Just as war will reward the victor less than it penalises the vanquished, so the world must, in a sense, lose as a whole if it sacrifices consumption of other goods to armaments. But since no supranational authority can guarantee indefinite peace, each country will perceive a need to arm to prevent its wealth falling prey to others. The last problem raised by public goods is the question of fairness. One person is most unlikely to place the same value on a public good as another: for the pacifist, defence expenditure has indeed a negative value, as has the police force for a criminal. But it is not possible to compensate people who claim to derive little (or negative) benefit from them: for, if they could, everyone would be tempted to claim compensation, demand would be understated and the provision of public goods would once more depend on inadequate voluntary contributions. The unpleasant conclusion to which one is drawn is that individuals must be coerced into contributing towards public goods, the precise characteristics of which they may not understand, and the purpose of which they may even abhor.

In contemporary Britain, expenditure by the State on the public goods identified above — defence, law enforcement, certain aspects of public health, the gathering of information — is approximately one-seventh of the national income. To these must be added the small sums spent on fire and lighthouse services. Defence expenditure, soon to fall to little over 4 per cent of national income, is rather higher than the average in West

European countries (only France, Portugal and Sweden exceed this) and in
previous periods of peace (2½ per cent was the typical level in Britain for
most of the inter-war period, for example). But the rapid rearmament of
the Soviet Union, and increasing isolationism of the United States, suggest
that there is little scope for further economies, and, if anything, a growing
case for a larger military presence in West Germany and a stronger naval
counter-submarine force in home waters. Much will depend on the success
of attempts to secure a more even distribution of defence costs among the
countries of Western Europe, and to arrange a balanced mutual reduction
of conventional forces with the Warsaw Pact. In law enforcement there is a
powerful case for fewer and lighter prison sentences and substantial
increases in the incidence and rate of fines, and for simplifying legal
procedure wherever possible. The Exchequer cost of imprisonment is
reaching (at the time of writing) £5000 per prisoner per year, and the true
resource cost − since people are removed from the labour force − is much
higher still.

Other savings might include wider use of automatic fixed penalties (at
higher rates) for motoring offences, lower limits on barristers' fees from
legal aid, and extensions of the jurisdiction of the Small Claims Court and
of magistrates' courts to settle minor cases now heard in higher courts.
Public health expenditure presents no conspicuous example of waste;
indeed, in some fields (particularly preventive medicine) there are grounds
for suspecting that too little is spent. Expenditure on gathering information is hard to classify and isolate; it may be taken to include the costs of
diplomatic representation overseas, research establishments and grants, and
incentives for research and development given to private industry. Recent
investigations into some aspects of these activities have cast doubts on
their usefulness or size: expenditure on embassies appears incommensurate
with Britain's shrunken influence in world politics; scientific research in
the institutions of higher education is felt to be too fragmented, dispersed
too widely, and too remote from the visible needs of industry; within
industry too much is thought to be devoted to technical research and
development in aviation. These charges are singularly hard to appraise: the
benefits from the expenditures are speculative and never immediate, and
the activities themselves are often comprehensible only to those engaged in
them. But since all institutions tend to outlive the task for which they
were created, the prevailing air of scepticism is not unhealthy.

The role of the State is not confined to the provision of public goods,
as we have defined them. Often using local authorities as agents, the State
also provides a further range of goods and services which lie on the
borderline between public and private goods: pensions, unemployment
and sickness insurance, medical facilities to cure incommunicable illness,
education, libraries, museums, parks, housing, and the road network. All
of these goods could be (and often are) provided privately in the market
place; but most give rise to some favourable external effect, and may be
termed 'quasi-public goods'.

The major problems confronting the Government in this area have been the determination of the appropriate level of expenditure – given the conflicting claims on its scarce resources – and how output and productivity can be monitored. The approach has often been intuitive, with heavy reliance placed on the political antennae of the members of the political party in power. Pensions, and unemployment and sickness benefits, are kept in approximate line with average earnings. One highly undesirable characteristic of State pensions – that they were subject to an earnings limit on the part of the recipient – is now fortunately being removed. A pension is the return on a lifetime's (involuntary) savings, and the State could have no justification in confiscating it. The limit also penalised those who wished to work, and deprived society of the fruits of the labour they would otherwise have given. On the other hand, the enforcement of compulsory contributions for National Insurance can be defended on the argument that some people need to be protected against their defective foresight in failing to provide adequately for their old age.

There is some case for allowing income tax deductibility (at the standard rate) for expenditure on private health insurance, and private education. The present Labour Government seems set upon a policy of gradual euthanasia for private medicine, and may well follow up its imposition of universal comprehensivisation on the state sector of secondary education with a concerted *jihad* against private schools. Yet, for balance of payments reasons, it seems keen to preserve the vestiges of the private system for foreigners. One is reminded of the luxury shops in Eastern Europe where goods may be purchased only with foreign exchange! The invasion of liberties that such policies represent is intelligible only as an ugly form of class warfare; in economic terms, it can only increase the costs the Exchequer bears. Education and the social services are discussed in detail elsewhere in this book; the only remaining economic point of note which does deserve emphasis here is the fact that productivity in these social services seems to have risen – if at all – far more slowly than in the provision of other goods and services. A conscious policy decision was taken in the 1950s and 1960s to lower the pupil/teacher ratio in schools, and to supplement teachers with an increasing number of non-teaching staff. Similar, if less pronounced, changes have occurred in other public services. The upshot of this has been an increased burden of tax on everyone, and not least the employees and owners of private firms. Pay in the public services has not lagged behind that in the private sector; if anything, there is some evidence that the reverse is true [*National Institute Economic Review*, number 74, November 1975, pp. 60–70] – at least in the period 1972–5. So, as the proportion of employees in the public services increases, the overall growth rate of real income declines – unless productivity increases at an accelerating rate in the rest of the economy. There are no grounds for such optimism. A measure of the importance of this effect is the change in the implicit cost of public authorities' current expenditure (per unit of output) in relation to the implicit cost per unit of all other components of gross national product, if one accepts the assumption generally made in national income accounts that productivity in the former is constant.

Before we turn to the nationalised industries — nationalised or about to be nationalised — one last component of government expenditure requires particular analysis: housing. Housing subsidies rose in money terms from £136 million in 1964 to £729 million in 1974; in real terms, there was a rise of 120 per cent in the four years from 1970/71, nearly all of which occurred in 1974. There has been a similar increase in the effective tax subsidy to house-buyers. There is an overwhelming case for permitting the sale of council houses to sitting tenants; it is scandalous that 30 per cent of the population should be kept in a state of landless helotry. Other possible reforms that merit consideration include the restoration of the 1970 real value of the average council rent, coupled with more generous rebates for low-income families; and a sharp reduction in the tax subsidy for owner-occupants. It is interesting to contrast the different tax treatment of buying shares, and buying a house. Borrowing for the former is not tax-deductible, but the latter is. Capital gains tax is levied on the former, but generally not the latter. Dividends are taxed, while the imputed rent of owner-occupied property is exempt. The only tax which goes some way to compensate for this distortion is household rates, which are worth preserving to lessen the unfavourable effects of government's housing policies upon the mobility of labour; in this respect, possibly the greatest single cause of the geographical arthritis of the labour force has been the steady decline in the private-rented sector of the housing market.

The experience of Britain's nationalised industries shows clearly how much less it matters *which* activities the State assumes than how well it carries them out. In ideal circumstances, decisions taken in nationalised industries should approximate as closely as possible to what they would have been in a perfect free market; whether the industry happens to be in public ownership makes no formal difference at all. In practice, however, the record of British nationalised industries — on any relevant criterion — has been variable, and there are several examples of mistakes attributable to the well-intentioned but misguided policy directives of the Government.

The nationalised activities can be divided into two groups: those experiencing rapid growth in demand (electricity, gas, telephones, airways) and the declining or stagnant giants (railways, coal, steel, postal services, bus services; British Leyland, soon to be joined in all probability by shipbuilding, and aerospace). On any yardstick one selects (the growth of output per employee, the sophistication of pricing decisions, the profit and loss accounts) there are pronounced differences between the two groups. The common difficulty confronting the second group has been the size of the wage bill in relation to operating receipts. Pay rises have outstripped the growth of productivity by a larger margin than in other industries, public or private; overmanning has remained chronic in most cases, despite a rapid rundown of the labour force in the 1960s in some of the industries concerned. But it must be emphasised that these problems have been no less evident in several other comparable countries, and are not attributable to nationalisation as such. Furthermore, there are even some reasons for expecting that some nationalised industries will (and should) earn a lower return on capital than is general in the private sector. It has now become accepted that large private firms facing bankruptcy should sometimes be nationalised instead; this may permit a more orderly rundown or rearrangement of their activities. The implication is that if the State acquires the ailing elements of the private sector, it can hardly be expected to earn levels of profit similar to those in enterprises which survive in private hands. Secondly, technical indivisibilities – which are particularly marked in the nationalised transport and telecommunications industries – justify low prices when demand is below peak, and it may be impractical to recoup the fixed costs in other ways. Thirdly, commercial profit may understate social gain: one thinks of the prohibitive increase in environmental costs that would result from closing some loss-making commuter railway lines (or even from charging break-even fares, if this were possible).

A number of policy changes would, none the less, be advantageous. Statutory monopolies in postal and bus services could be removed. Huge tracts of urban wasteland owned by nationalised industries (particularly British Rail) could be released for housing, industry and commerce. The principle of natural wastage, to trim employment in industries where overmanning is serious, could be restored; it was unhappily laid aside too often in the early 1970s. Nationalised industries could be required to publish forecasts annually of output and employment over the subsequent decade, and, where appropriate, adhere to a programme of continuous falls in employment.

Government intervention in the nationalised industries has often been myopic in recent years. The industries have been asked to cancel or augment projects for investment on a number of occasions, for general macroeconomic purposes of questionable merit. Investment projects themselves have been subject to appraisal, but the Test Discount Rate employed to calculate their current value (now 10 per cent) has been excessive – the estimates of future net receipts are expressed in constant prices – and there has been a consequent bias against projects with long lives. At best a high Test Discount Rate is likely to be a distorting way of correcting for excessive optimism on the part of those estimating the future earnings of such projects. At worst, it can lead to severe misallocation of resources. Another instance of injudicious intervention by central Government was the instruction to the nationalised industries to contain price rises far beneath the rises in their costs. This began in 1971, and became significant in 1973 and 1974. It led to an explosion in subsidies, as 'compensation for price restraint'. It played an important role in the deterioration of the public finances. The underlying logic behind the feverish attempt to suppress some of the symptoms of inflation is quite unconvincing. Such mistakes should not be repeated.

Still more alarming is the attachment of much of the Labour Party to the 'museum economy': the belief that enterprises producing goods for a disappearing market should be preserved as long as possible in their present state. No doctrine poses a greater threat to the future living standards of the British people as a whole. If it is to guide policy towards industries now undergoing, or likely to undergo, nationalisation, the long-term effects will be disastrous. In shipbuilding and vehicle assembly, overmanning has been the besetting problem. International comparisons of productivity show the UK in a very poor light. Overmanning has held down the real earnings of the employees in the industry. It has also led to such a high share of total earnings being absorbed by the wage bill that the firms concerned could generate very little retained earnings for capital expansion; and in the circumstances, external finance has also proved very hard to obtain. Low investment has compounded the problem of low productivity and, when aggravated by delivery delays, led to still further falls in the British producers' share of the international market for the products. Trade unions, aware of the threat to the jobs of their members have quite understandably not exercised themselves to speed up the rate of work; but this, of course, reinforces the underlying problem of overmanning. The 1973–6 recession, and the sharp rise in interest rates facing companies in debt, determined only the timing of British Leyland's collapse. Shipbuilding has been insulated (temporarily) by mounting Government subsidies, order backlogs and North Sea oil work; but prospects for the end of the decade are very bleak. Large-scale surgery is needed in both these industries. Temporising loans with minimal prospect of repayment are no substitute for generous arrangements for the voluntary severance of employment, natural wastage, and the orderly creation of alternative jobs. The free market solution (resale to private enterprise) merits consideration in the more distant future; but it is hard to see how the State can avoid deep involvement of some kind in these industries in the period of their transition to higher levels of productivity.

Aerospace is also likely — at the time of writing — to undergo nationalisation. The problems in this industry are purely of the Government's making. Despite Treasury scepticism and opposition, Governments have ordered and financed a sorry string of loss-making aviation projects. The last and most expensive of these is Concorde. The Concorde project came close to cancellation on a number of occasions (1964, 1967, 1971), only to be saved by two arguments: so much had already been spent; and our French collaborators would try to exact a high penalty (possibly a further veto on our application for the membership of the EEC). Of these, the second was more telling: present choices should be made independently of past mistakes. The British share of Concorde's development costs amounts to some £750 million in 1976 prices. Receipts from confirmed orders will probably not even cover production costs, let alone contribute anything towards development costs. The project is not without some 'external' benefits, whether technological or even aesthetic; but it is hard to avoid the conclusion that Concorde represents the most wasteful single commitment into which a British Government has ever entered. Some picture of what has been sacrificed as a result can be obtained from these considerations: the total development costs are equal to about one-thirteenth of the total annual yield of income tax, at current rates; they are 25 times greater than the annual budget of the Medical Research Council; probably at least 100 times greater than the combined cost of saving York Minster and Canterbury Cathedral; and several hundred times greater than the initial costs of developing hovercraft. Nationalisation of the aerospace industries has nothing to commend it; indeed, one must bemoan the risk that some of their operations will be removed still further from the realm of commercial sanity.

The 1975 Community Land Act extended public ownership into development land. This marks the first occasion when nationalisation became genuinely confiscatory. Hitherto, the former owners of national-ised assets have had to sell at prices based on market valuation; in the case of development land, owners will be made to sell at existing use value, and the local authorities (who are to implement the provisions of the Act) will then be free to sell at the value augmented by the conferment of planning permission. The gain accrues to the local authority. One is confronted with two arguments for the Act: the redistributive case that the State confers value by according planning permission, and should distribute this gain to everyone; and the economic hypothesis that the shortage of land and housing is due to speculative hoarding by private landowners. The redistributive case would command more respect if there were no Capital Gains Tax payable on land, and no corporation or Income Tax payable on rents. The tax system already taxes development gains quite severely and there is no acceptable case for the wholesale expropriation which the Act permits. The second hypothesis − that speculators are to blame for the shortages − does not stand up to analysis. Speculators do not aim to sit on their holdings indefinitely; they aim to make profits by selling at a higher price than that at which they bought. If they succeed in making profits, their activities will (more often than not) tend to *reduce the swings* in the prices of the assets in which they deal, and have no overall effect on the trend in the price of those assets. It can be maintained, with some justification, that the shortages of housing and building land − so far from contributing a case for further Government intervention − are largely the result of mistaken Government intervention in the past.

It is to the redistributive role of Government that we turn next. What all these secondary economic 'interventions' by the State have in common

is the underlying rationalisation that, left to itself, the free market is liable
to failure. The way it parcels out income between persons and families
depends on the economic power of the work groups to which individuals
belong, on energy, skill, inheritance, accumulated savings and luck.
Attitudes to inequality have changed; ironically, as inequality has fallen in
recent decades, it has appeared increasingly unpalatable to the majority of
the British people. The gradual process of equalisation in incomes has been
abetted by redistributive taxation; the two World Wars were particularly
important, since both were accompanied by sharp increases in marginal
rates of income tax, especially on high incomes, which were only slightly
offset by subsequent falls. There are only minor differences between the
records of past peacetime Conservative and Labour Governments on
redistributive taxation; the former have often lowered the standard rate of
income tax slightly (which brings higher proportionate rises in after-tax
income to high-income earners than low-income earners), and brought
down the top marginal rates on the highest incomes; Labour Governments
have usually done little more than restore the previous Conservative
Government's cuts. Both have extended benefits in cash and goods to the
worse off, with Conservative Governments preferring to concentrate
assistance on those with the lowest incomes, with emphasis on pecuniary
transfers, while Labour has shown a predilection for uniform, non-selective
welfare benefits in kind.

Income tax is not without disadvantages. It inevitably distorts choices
between leisure and other goods, even if (as could happen) this has
negligible effect on the hours of work. Furthermore, if income tax is to be
progressive, so that the average rate of tax increases with income, the
marginal rate must exceed the average rate; and high marginal rates have
deleterious effects on the mobility of labour between occupations, and on
incentives. The higher the marginal rate of tax, the more closely the
individual's leisure approximates to a public bad: everyone is made to bear
the cost of each hour any individual chooses not to work. We are
confronted once more by the prisoners' dilemma. Society has a complicated choice to make: efficiency, liberty and equality are, it appears,
not naturally compatible if individuals differ in skill and earning power.
Coercion, and the direction of labour, will enable society to secure both
efficiency and equality; liberty and efficiency can be attained (in
otherwise ideal conditions) if marginal income taxation is removed, but if
income tax is to all but equalise incomes (implying marginal rates close to
100 per cent in a social system which permits individuals to choose
whether, where and how long to work), the economy will disintegrate and
even the poorest will suffer. In practice, of course, Governments must
secure some balance between coercion, inequality and economic collapse;
if coercion is discountenanced, there must surely be a strong case for
lowering marginal tax rates from their present maximum of 83 per cent on
the highest earned incomes, to nearer 70 per cent (the approximate

average of the highest rates in France, West Germany and the United States); and for reducing the 'clawback' of means-tested benefits (rent and rate rebates, family income supplement, school meals charges and so on) which at present can make the effective marginal rate of income tax approach, and even exceed, 100 per cent on some low incomes.

Inequality of wealth, and of the income derived from it, is more pronounced than inequality of income in general. Inequality of wealth has shown some tendency to fall: the percentage of total personal wealth owned by the richest 1 per cent in Great Britain fell, according to a recent estimate, from 55 per cent to 31 per cent between 1938 and 1968, while the share of the richest 5 per cent went down from 78 per cent to 56 per cent over the period. In contrast, the top 10 per cent of income recipients in the United Kingdom were calculated to have received 28 per cent of total income before tax, and 24.3 per cent of total income after tax, over the period 1949–67. Despite increasingly severe rates of estate duty (payable on death) over the past eighty years, the Exchequer's yield from death duties has been surprisingly low (usually little over ½ per cent of national income each year, and approximately one-third of the yield one would expect on an actuarial basis). The reasons for this have been the opportunities afforded hitherto by gifts *inter vivos*, trusts and favourable probate valuation of land, for the rich to escape much of the tax when transmitting wealth to their heirs. The Labour Government's capital transfer tax (introduced in 1974–5 to replace death duties) is to be welcomed in that many of the loopholes have been closed without any sizeable change in the expected yield. But the wealth tax it proposes to introduce in 1977 is an entirely different matter. Virtually all forms in which wealth is held yield income which is liable to tax. Which is preferable: a tax on the stock of wealth or on the flow of income? The costs of administration, valuation and collection are undoubtedly lower in the second case. It is true that assets do not all yield the same pecuniary income; so a *prima facie* case for a wealth tax can be based on the view that unearned income tax can be in part avoided by acquiring low-yielding assets. But on inspection, this case is weaker than it appears. Low-income assets bear low yield usually because they are expected to appreciate in value; if expectations are fulfilled, the capital gain will be taxed on realisation. Real estate is liable to rates. Retained earnings in companies are liable to corporation tax, now at 52 per cent. *Objets d'art* bear no income, but they are liable to capital gains tax if their vendor declares their value; and what guarantee can there be that he will declare their true value if a wealth tax is imposed? Stamp duty catches asset-holders who time their purchases and sales to avoid dividends. Existing loopholes like split-level trusts can be closed by imaginative legislation. Since taxation on property income can be made virtually equivalent to taxation on wealth, at considerably lower cost, the case against a wealth tax is overwhelming.

The Government's *macroeconomic* involvements have a long history. At an early stage in social evolution, the Sovereign assumes control of the issue of commodity money. Circulating coins are stamped with his image or badge. Later, token claims on metallic money are introduced. Inflation can develop if the coinage is debased or the token claims are increased; both are disguised forms of taxation, to which resort is made in periods of exceptional fiscal strain. In the simplest versions of 'monetarism', the macroeconomic responsibilities of the Government begin and end with its obligation to keep control of the supply of money. Needless to say, the problems of macroeconomic policy have long ago acquired greater complexity than this.

Inflation is not the only *macroeconomic* misfortune with which a country may become afflicted. There are, broadly, three others. First, there can be fluctuations in the general level of national income in real terms – in the purchasing power of the aggregate of each individual's income. Fluctuations in this can induce fluctuations in unemployment, in the opposite direction. Second, the country can experience difficulties in the balance of its external payments (the record of transactions between its residents and foreign residents). Lastly, the country's real national income may grow at what is thought to be an unsatisfactory rate.

These four objectives – the *stabilisation of aggregate demand* at some appropriate level (generally as close as possible to what is known as productive potential), the *avoidance of inflation, balance in external payments*, and a *satisfactory growth rate* – are all areas of legitimate public concern. Governments, in consequence, have assumed responsibility for them. The four objectives are hard to reconcile, since performances on each score are interrelated: the reduction of inflation may entail a rise in unemployment, and a fall in companies' investment expenditure which will react unfavourably on the growth of productive potential; a change in the growth rate may entail an adverse movement in the balance of payments; and so on. There are sound reasons for thinking that a policy of *laissez-faire* will often fail to achieve these objectives, or at least fail to achieve them with sufficient speed.

We examine the first two of these objectives in turn. First, the stabilisation of aggregate demand. The Government's role here is based on two propositions: one, booms and slumps can develop spontaneously; two, the Government has the means to even out these fluctuations. The argument in support of proposition one runs as follows. The expenditure plans of companies and households can change of their own accord. Expectations of future income and future profit from investment are not constant. The timing of purchases is not constant – particularly for purchases of assets (plant, machinery, consumer durables). Prices are observed to move little when there are changes in aggregate expenditure decisions; or, to be more precise, prices move little to start with in markets for manufactured products, and tend to be especially inflexible downwards. So the response is seen, at least in part, in the levels of production (and employment).

Proposition two is easily established. The Government possesses an armoury of financial weapons which can influence aggregate expenditure. The State can alter its own expenditure. Tax rates (on income or expenditure or profits) can be altered, with consequent effects on the spending of households and companies. The supply of money — nowadays dominated by the 'inside' money created by the banking system — can be altered by changing the reserves of the banks which form the base of their deposit-taking and lending operations. In this way and others, the terms and amount of credit can be changed — credit used to finance much of the most volatile components of the private sector's expenditure.

Yet the record of post-war Governments on stabilisation has proved rather dismal. Most recent studies have concluded that Government financial policies have probably, on balance, added to the fluctuations in aggregate demand. The reason for this has not been inadequate forecasts of how demand would move if no policy actions were taken, so much as excessive reaction to lagged indicators. The story has been 'too much, too late'. Unemployment rises when aggregate demand turns down, relative to its trend; but it reacts with a lag of up to a year. So unemployment reaches its peak usually three or four quarters after the trough of the business cycle. Mindful of an election that may be pending in a year or two's time, Governments bow to political pressure and reflate demand when the upswing has already begun. The instruments of reflation have lagged effects — the maximum impact on demand may not be felt for as much as twelve or eighteen months — so the economy is driven rapidly into supply shortages, a burgeoning import bill, and an inflation or balance of payments crisis. Two or three quarters after the business cycle peak, there is likely to be a major outflow on the balance of payments: the trade figures show a substantial and persistent deficit, and confidence in sterling cracks. The Government then reacts by restricting demand, strengthening the deflationary forces already at work. This depressing pattern has been evident for most of the period since 1950. Government expenditure seems to have had something of a stabilising effect on the business cycle; it has been the other financial instruments the use of which has been mistimed — swings in the rate of growth of the money supply, discretionary tax changes, and, above all, changes in the regulations affecting the hire-purchase of consumer durables.

Yet it would be rash to conclude that Governments should abrogate the discretionary use of financial instruments to affect aggregate demand. The regular and rather mild business cycle of the post-war period, which has displayed an interval between peaks of about 54 months, could easily become severer in future; indeed, the first half of the 1970s shows a marked increase in the violence of swings, which is partly attributable to its growing international synchronisation. It is too early to pass judgement on the monetarist contention that actual cycles in the past would have been ironed out had the growth in the money supply been held constant; it is true that these cycles have usually been preceded by cycles in the money supply relative to its trend – but the correlation is far from perfect, and the question of which caused which still remains open. The Government must, therefore, stand ready to use its financial instruments to stabilise aggregate demand; but it must use them with greater intelligence – earlier and less fiercely – than it has done in the past.

The second macroeconomic objective is the avoidance of inflation. The public is presented with a number of competing explanations of the genesis of inflation, and no fewer distinct policy prescriptions for its removal. The monetarist view is that inflation is *by definition* impossible in an economy in which transactions occur by barter, rather than through the medium of money; that an increase in the money supply (temporarily) augments people's spending power, which tends to raise the demand for everything; and that prices rise to choke off the extra demand unless extra resources can be brought into play to raise the supplies of the commodities, or assets, or factors in excess demand. The policy prescription is simple: curtail the growth of money. The sociological view is that inflation registers incompatible claims on the national product – in particular, but not exclusively, the claims of labour. Incomes policy is recommended for its control and elimination. Yet others stress the growth of Government spending, or expectations of inflation which may become self-fulfilling, or depreciations in the exchange rate. Still other explanations contain elements of at least two of the mechanisms already described.

It is the mongrel approach which best fits the bewildering variety of inflations experienced. Such econometric evidence as exists suggests that none of the given possibilities (money-push, wage-push, Government spending-push, expectations-push, exchange rate-push) can be discounted, and indeed that all of the mechanisms are likely to be intertwined. The money-push hypothesis fell out of fashion for at least three decades after the publication in 1936 of Keynes's *General Theory of Interest, Employment and Money*; the arguments for the alleged impotence of monetary changes have now come to look very ragged under the mounting weight of theoretical and empirical findings against them. But the crucial question is not 'Has this inflation been accompanied (or preceded) by changes in the money supply?' but 'Why did this increase in the money supply come about?' There are many different answers to this: sometimes because the Government wanted to lower the unemployment which has arisen from over-rapid wage rises in earlier quarters; sometimes because it hoped to escape some of the costs of servicing its (growing) debts; sometimes because it wished to boost investment, or avoid bankruptcies;

sometimes because of processes in the banking system it could not or would not interrupt.

Turning to the labour market, we are confronted with a glaring example of the prisoners' dilemma. If one group of workers secures a pay rise, everyone else may suffer from the rise in price of the good they produce. But all the beneficiaries need fear is the increased chance of unemployment − a slim one, of course, if it is thought likely that the Government may 'underpin' the pay rise by loans or allowances to the employer, or by general macroeconomic reflation. Yet, collectively, workers will dislike inflation and the increased social tensions and financial nuisances that it brings. Wage rises are a public bad and a private good. Furthermore, workers are often at least as concerned with their position in the wage hierarchy as with their real wages; and given that wages are not renegotiated continuously, inflation brings with it rapid oscillations in the wage hierarchy, and possibly also greater information on the level and movement of differentials.

Perhaps the most cogent evidence for placing some emphasis on wages as a prime mover in the inflationary process is the rapid fall in the profit share of national income that has occurred in the decade of inflation take-off, 1965−75. One would expect demand inflation to be associated with rises, not falls, in the profit share. The trend increase in unemployment seems to point in the same direction − to a wage-push explanation. Yet the 'permissive' monetary policy of Governments must also have played a role, and there are good reasons for thinking that the wage rises in 1974 and 1975 would have been much lower had it not been for the monetary and fiscal expansion of 1971−3, and the effect of the sinking of sterling on perceptions and expectations of changes in the domestic retail price index.

Just as unicausal explanations of inflation appear theoretically unsound and disconsonant with the facts, simple policy prescriptions for its eradication are likely to be dangerous. Rapid reductions in the growth of the money supply impose arbitrary and savage bankruptcies and will only slow downwards pressure on the rate of rise of wages. Incomes policies work most easily when substantial unemployment has rendered them less necessary; they pose grave problems of anomalies; if they fossilise wage differentials, they impede resource reallocation in a period of structural change; evidence suggests that it is their initial effect which is strongest, and that political and economic pressures often make them almost unworkable after more than 12 or 18 months. Most inadvisable of all is the error into which many Governments have fallen: the belief that inflation is cured by issuing edicts against rises in the prices of particular goods. This confuses the causes of inflation with its symptoms; it leads to violent changes in the price ratios between different goods, with probable consequent losses in efficiency; by cutting production and raising demand

for certain commodities, it may impose adverse effects on the balance of
payments — and this, if the exchange rate is floating, can aggravate
inflation itself; when applied to the products of nationalised industries, or
to goods on which heavy indirect tax is levied and for which demand is
inelastic, it will increase the budget deficit — and this, too, can be
inflationary if steps are not taken to block any increase in the money
supply that would otherwise result.

If (and in so far as) one is led to agree that wage control is a
prerequisite for attacking inflation — and even the pure monetarist and
Government spending theories require this, at least for the wage bill for
public employees — the co-operation or acquiescence of organised labour
is essential. The Conservative Party has rightly prided itself on realism
about the true centres of power; not for Conservatives the Utopian flights
of fancy so characteristic of the British left. Euripides writes of the
flexible tree which bends with the wind and withstands the storm;
statecraft amounts to knowing when and how far to yield. The events of
the winter of 1973—4 will prove to have effects on the subsequent course
of British history as profound as any since the Second World War. The
embargo and price explosion of oil demonstrated the fragility of the
advanced economy based on transforming primary products into sophisticated manufactures; the miners' strike, the fragility of Britain's social
relations. The Conservative Party must construct a firm and credible
concordat with those unions representing the monopolistic aristocracies of
labour which could demonstrate the indispensability of their members'
services; otherwise it is doomed to oblivion.

No less important than the task of reducing inflation is that of
correcting its effects. If one country experiences faster inflation than
others, its balance of payments — perhaps after a lag — will deteriorate; so
its exchange rate must sink for competitiveness in international markets to
be restored. But it is the domestic effects of inflation which are liable to
cause greatest anxiety. Unexpectedly rapid inflation transfers wealth from
those who have lent in financial contracts to their debtors; unexpectedly
slow inflation redistributes in the other direction. Money is the normal
standard of deferred payment; but uncertainty about the rate of inflation
makes contracts denominated in money distinctly dangerous — for both
lenders and borrowers. In a very minor way, the Labour Government has
moved tentatively towards providing inflation-proofed savings media: the
index-linked Save-as-you-Earn contracts, and the £500 bonds available to
old age pensioners, are the first steps in what one must hope will be a
major process of indexing large slices of the Government's debt. The legal
and fiscal obstacles to the indexation of company debentures, life
insurance contracts and other financial instruments must be removed at
the earliest opportunity. Indexation would enable borrowers to phase the
real burden of amortisation more evenly; it could succeed in *lowering* the
costs of servicing the National Debt if one accepts that 'unprotected'

bonds would sell at a discount against equivalent indexed bonds; it would restore tranquility to capital markets which have been gravely shaken by the events of the period 1973–6. The strange effects of inflation on the Government's budget could be removed by indexing overdue tax, by replacing specific duties with *ad valorem* taxes, and by indexing the thresholds at which different rates of income tax apply. Indexation is not to be seen as a substitute for counter-inflation policy, but a useful complement to it.

Space precludes discussion of the other macroeconomic tasks that Governments have assumed (managing external payments, and attempting to select an appropriate growth rate).

What can be concluded from this brief *tour d'horizon* of the major economic roles of the State? First and foremost, the State will not wither away; in many of its functions, it is indispensable; one may dispute the merits of actual decisions taken, but not its right to take them. On the other hand, there are some areas — of which housing is the most prominent example — where the case for State intervention on its present scale is very weak, and where particularly myopic policies have been applied. 'Good in parts, my Lord', said the curate, when asked to deliver judgement on the egg he was eating for breakfast. This must be our judgement, too.

6 Managing the Economy

JOHN REDWOOD

Local and national government expenditure, the nationalised industries' claims upon the consolidated and the national loans funds, together with government-financed transfer incomes, account for nearly 60 per cent of the gross national product of the United Kingdom. Consequently, government decisions must and do affect the overall levels of activity in the country, and any Government is forced to take decisions in the public sector which influence the economy as a whole. Six of the largest corporations in the United Kingdom are nationalised near-monopoly industries, controlling the energy, transportation and commmunications sectors of our economy. Nationalised enterprises have a joint turnover of over £10,500 million a year, and the influence of nationalisation is now being extended into the steel and engineering sectors of the economy. National government wields extensive powers by regulative legislation, taxation of income and capital, and by its power to call upon resources to finance the social services, education, defence, environmental policies, law and order and industrial policy. Local authorities, through rate support grants, rates and charges, stake their claim to over £13,000 million a year (1975 prices) of the country's money.

The Government should be concerned about two major and related problems. First, it is important for the economy as a whole that the powers of the public sector should be used to encourage efficiency, growth and full employment of the resources available in this country. Secondly, full employment of resources should not be achieved by creating an unreasonable\ distribution between public and private sectors, or between different economic activities. Such a misallocation of resources, like that created by massive revenue subsidisation of the nationalised industries or of public companies, may temporarily preserve employment in the nationalised sector and offers some transitory benefit to the consumer. In the medium term, however, private enterprise is starved of resources which it could deploy more successfully, the competitive position of the United Kingdom is adversely affected, the preservation of full employment becomes more difficult, and the policy of subsidisation results in more expense for both consumer and taxpayer alike. The large sums being paid to British Leyland and Chrysler may protect employment in those companies in the short term, but they contribute to inflation and unemployment elsewhere in the economy.

A successful market economy rests on allowing the market to

determine the prices charged and the volume of goods and services traded. Any government intervention in the form of subsidy payments to suppliers, or in the form of restrained prices, distorts the volume of activity between sectors. If, for example, the Government decides to subsidise car production, so that the customer pays less but the general taxpayer pays more, then demand for cars will be artificially increased, and resources will have to be diverted away from more viable activities to satisfy demand for cheap cars. This process of distortion can lead to declining economic performance, for resources are no longer concentrated on those goods which are in demand at an economic price and in which the economy may have a relative advantage against producers elsewhere in the world.

It is neither possible nor desirable to return to a free market economy. There would be too much upheaval involved in dismantling the large State and private monopolies currently operating in the economy. Some good does come from the economies of scale that can be enjoyed by monopoly or near-monopoly suppliers, e.g. producers of coal, water, electricity, rail travel, and other products. In addition, many goods are supplied at subsidised prices for social reasons, and it is part of our quality of life that free medicine and education, for example, should be available on demand. There are many missing markets, where people need goods and services, but cannot afford them, where humanity dictates the provision of a general public service. The market economy is not a satisfactory solution to all our problems over allocation, but the market price mechanism is an important one in determining resource allocation. Missing markets, particularly in the welfare and educational fields, do necessitate government intervention and expenditure, but it is rash to develop from this argument a belief that there is a missing market for practically everything.

The choice in broad economic strategy is a simple one. We can choose, if we so wish, to expand the scope of government activity at its present, or even at an increased rate. Such a policy will entail a narrowing choice for all of us in terms of goods we can buy, the suppliers we can call upon, the jobs we can obtain, the employers for whom we work, the power we have to vote with our purse, and the freedom we have to spend our own income. Alternatively, we can determine to impose limits to rightful government intervention in our economy and society. The first course entails a command economy, in which allocation occurs by rationing, and in which the variety thrown up by competition and freedom is pared away, to be replaced by the profligacies and inadequacies of State planning. To choose the second course entails accepting the need for Britain to remain competitive in world markets, to adapt to market forces, to preserve areas of choice free from political intervention, to retain risk and reward, incentive and initiative. It is impossible to have a public sector as large as our present public sector and growing at its current rate, without endangering the freedoms and the initiatives of all our people.

If recent policies are extrapolated the public sector will consume the whole of the gross domestic product before the end of this century. Even if gross domestic product grows at a rate of 2½ per cent a year for the next twenty-five years, and over the last two it has scarcely grown at all, public expenditure growing at 5 per cent per annum would overtake it before the year 2000. The ultimate constraint to increasing public expenditure is only reached when it can no longer absorb an increasing share of our national product, and when it is no longer possible to borrow overseas to finance public works and employment.

There will doubtless be periods of prosperity and boom between now and 2000, periods when the economy will grow more rapidly than at 2½ per cent per annum. It is equally true that in times when public expenditure is restrained the growth in real public expenditure will fall below 5 per cent as indicated by the latest White Paper plans. However, there is no reason to suppose that the overall rate of growth in the economy, if we take both boom and slump together over a twenty-five-year time span, will be any higher than 2½ per cent, given current attitudes towards productivity and growth and the many restraints which now operate in the British economy against achieving a more rapid rate of improvement in gross national product per head. It is only very recently that there has been some sign of firm intentions on the part of the Government to curb the claim on resources made by the public sector, which will continue to increase unless we now decide to limit its size. Had any forecast in 1963 suggested that public expenditure, which was then 43 per cent of the gross national product, would rise to 60 per cent in 1975, few would have accepted the prediction. Local authority expenditure, one of the most buoyant elements in total public expenditure, has been growing at 8 per cent a year in the early 1970s. There are many active and vocal lobbies still arguing their case on very reasonable and humane grounds, in favour of increasing the growth rate in local and national government expenditure. These attitudes, fostered by a belief that the State must and should provide for all people in all eventualities, are powerful forces in our society; they will be present over the ensuing years urging governments to spend more and more. In important areas like social service provision, we have to seek value for money and decide on priorities, as Ann Spokes cogently argues in her essay in favour of high-quality social provision helping those truly in need.

The distortions caused by too rapid a growth of public expenditure are reflected in many areas of activity. First, it is difficult to pursue sensible fiscal policies that do not restrain initiative and enterprise, when public expenditure requires large and ever-increasing sums to be raised from taxation. Secondly, monetary policy is difficult to manage in the interests of a sensible counter-inflation strategy, when the Government has to print money, and has to release a large number of Treasury bills into the banking system, thereby further augmenting the money supply through the creation of additional high-powered money. Thirdly, capital-raising in financial markets to finance productive investment is affected by the demands on financial markets to fund the public borrowing requirement. During the first half of 1975, when both the primary stock market and the gilt-edged market were functioning well, for every £1 that was subscribed to industry in ordinary share rights issues some £5 was subscribed for the Government in gilts by the non-banking sector. It is difficult for any Government to argue that institutional and private investors are unwilling or unable to finance the capital requirements of British industry, when much of their unwillingness is a figment of government's imagination, and much of their inability is the result of government profligacy. Fourthly, the competitive position of industry in world markets is affected by the increased costs of materials, products and labour resulting both from the higher incidence of taxation necessitated by heavy government expenditure programmes, and from the inflation generated by the lack of control over money supply which results from such a policy.

It is essential to curb the rate of growth in the public sector and to seek more effective use of our resources. The policies required are not easy to implement, as they involve a restoration of financial disciplines and a reversal of so many assumptions fostered by the splurge of public spending in 1974 and 1975. They are policies which are easily misrepresented, their critics arguing that they involve short-term unemployment of an unacceptably high order and a deterioration in many of the public services which have become correctly revered on both sides of the House of Commons.

It is important to spell out in any programme of public expenditure restraint that the aim of the policy is not to create a worse health service for the sick and elderly, or a worse education service for our children. Nor is the aim of the policy to see financial disciplines resulting in massive unemployment in nationalised industries and other public services. Proper public expenditure control is not designed to create a large dole queue of civil servants, teachers and social workers. What is required instead is primarily that the nationalised industries should be left to their own devices in running the services awarded to them. The nationalised industries' managements and men should respond to the demand of their consumers, and should manage their own finances in such a way as to obviate the need for recourse to public financial aid. Their capital expenditure should be financed out of their own resources, or through borrowing from the market by issues of loan stocks on competitive coupons. An immediate reduction in publicly financed activity could be achieved by phasing out the revenue subsidies to nationalised industries which have amounted to vast and almost unbelievable sums of money over the past two years. The table illustrates the size of the problem, and the scope for improvement which would result from setting the nationalised industries free to pursue their own market strategies and to balance their own budgets.

The nationalised industries, 1974/75 (£m.)

	Turnover	Loss [Profit]	Grants	Tax
National Coal Board	1589.6	3.9	68.2	1.2
Post Office	2122.67	306.66	–	–
Gas Council	1206.7	44.1	–	0.1
Electricity Council	2434.9	257.6	–	–
British Steel Corporation	2255.8	[89.3]	39.0	40.9
British Rail	914.9	157.8	154.2	–
Total	10,524.57	680.76	261.4	42.2

In addition to reviewing the nationalised industries and their financing, it is essential to review the scope of functions at present undertaken by central government departments and local authorities. Government over the last fifteen years has grown at a terrifying rate, so much so that the levels of manning in both local and central government have had to increase very rapidly in order to keep pace with the extension of functions. Local government reorganisation, which should have brought greater efficiency and some streamlining, brought instead a huge increase in expenditure on overheads. The restoration of balance in the economy between public and private, government and individual, would require a reduction in the number of functions and responsibilities undertaken by local and national authorities, and any new Government must avoid enacting legislation which places further responsibilities upon public bodies. It is now accepted practice, and desirably so, that government should run an education service, and that a National Health Service should be provided free and on demand. But is is debatable whether government should attempt to run bus and railway services, whether it should police trading practices, or employ thousands of people in acquiring land under compulsory purchase orders to implement the Community Land legislation, together with thousands of people in planning, forecasting and monitoring most of our activities. In many fields of human activity from housing to the provision of leisure facilities, from transport to planning, there is ample room for reducing the role of government without impoverishing the quality of life.

The best method of restraining public expenditure is to reduce the functions of government and to grant independence to nationalised industries. In addition, it will be necessary to review the way in which government and public authorities carry out their present duties and to investigate allegations of overmanning, inefficiency, and lack of management control. It is impossible without access to the books of specific authorities, and without day-to-day knowledge of their management, to decide whether any major economies would materialise. But in the present author's experience the scope for reducing the fat in local government, which results both from duplication of function between County and District and from over-zealous recruitment, is very considerable.

All of these policies designed to restore some balance between competing claims on resources must proceed in conjuction with an overall strategy capable of tackling the twin central problems of inflation and unemployment. Inflation is a major problem in any economy. Vast and accelerating rates of inflation breed inflationary expectations. Tax revenue increases in so far as wages bring in higher tax receipts, but fiscal drag usually fails to keep pace with growing government expenditure. The effect of inflation on corporate liquidity is to squeeze corporate profits and therefore limit the flows from corporation tax. Wage inflation in the public sector outstrips available resources, and leads to larger financial deficits and recourse to increased money supply to meet the outgoings required to maintain services. Financial constraints on public expenditure imposed through real growth targets become meaningless when the cash outflows to finance inflation exceed the real growth rates by a factor of 10 or more. High rates of inflation make the over-run of real growth rates by public authorities so much the easier, whilst the effects of an accelerating inflation consequent upon it are visible in the redistribution of wealth between borrowers and lenders, high nominal interest rates, pressure on companies through higher working capital requirements, penalisation of anyone on a fixed or sticky income, and the difficulty of remunerating the higher paid to give them any recompense at the net level in a rigid system of high marginal rates in a progressive tax structure.

An accelerating inflation enriches certain sections of the community, especially borrowers and strongly placed unions, at the expense of others, especially savers and those on fixed incomes and pensions. The level of housing and transport subsidy awarded to those in public housing and those using bus and train travel escalates rapidly. The level of tax on the ratepayer and income-earner increases disproportionately. The real money supply may well fall, causing recessionary forces to build up, at the same time that the accelerating nominal money supply adds further fuel to inflation. The result is maldistribution of scarce resources, economic uncertainty and ultimately contraction, with the painful loss of jobs that that inevitably generates.

Most people would agree that inflation in double or treble figures per year is undesirable because of these distortions, and the effect that they ultimately have on the level of activity. The causes of this phenomenon, and the policies necessary to correct it have, however, been a matter of serious controversy. In the 1960s the debate was largely one over the relative importance of demand-pull and cost-push forces: in the 1970s there has been an equally significant debate between monetarists and so-called neo-Keynesians.

Broadly these disputes have been concerned either with the underlying cause or first mover of inflation, or with locating an essential force which could be subject to political control and would of itself cure the problem. Thus those who argued that inflation was basically caused by demand-pull, believed that a government had only to reduce the level of demand in the economy through tax increases or expenditure cuts in order to reduce the level of inflation. Such a policy would, it was argued, automatically curb cost-push as the volume of resources demanded would reduce and the prices would therefore weaken or cease to rise so rapidly.

Those who adhered to the cost-push theory argued a position similar to that adopted by the neo-Keynesians, that free collective bargaining pushed up wage rates, which were the prime cause of inflation in the economy.

The debate was inconclusive, but it was often asking the largely uninteresting question of what was the first cause, rather than asking the more relevant question of what policies, given that both demand and cost elements were involved in the process, could be successfully implemented and would be sufficient to control both elements in the spiral. The more recent debate has centred upon whether or not price levels can be controlled merely by controlling the money supply. Those of a sociological bent of mind argue that trade union attitudes, or excess demand or expectations, are phenomena independent of money aggregates. The monetarists counter by arguing that control of the money supply can solve the inflationary problem by forcing a choice between more cash and more activity.

Policy monetarists often concentrate on the rate of growth in M3, the measure of the money supply which includes currency, current accounts, deposit accounts and Certificates of Deposit. They argue that control over the printing presses and over the banking system is sufficient to control inflation.

The resolution of these debates is germane to policy discussion. Demand-pull theorists and monetarists would both argue that an incomes policy is a false response to wage inflation, which could be attributed either to demand for labour and materials in excess of the supply or to excessive money supply growth. Neo-Keynesians would argue that control over money aggregates cannot of itself cure a sociological phenomenon, and may in its wake bring other ills like a high rate of unemployment.

Any crude dichotomy of view oversimplifies both the problem with which the views are trying to deal, and the debate itself. Even Milton Friedman, the apostle of the new monetarists, would accept in his more mature and complex work that forces other than money supply factors are important in an inflationary spiral. He would agree that one of the major problems is those forces which lead to an increase in the money supply, and would accept that an increase in the money supply is not always an independent variable deliberately created by governments wishing to pursue excessive expenditure policies. In addition, he and the monetarists have to accept that the velocity of circulation of money varies as does the quantity of money in circulation, and that the velocity often reinforces a boom or a slump by rising or falling as the inflationary or recessionary forces gain momentum. Similarly, the neo-Keynesians, concentrating upon sociological and other features more than the Friedmanites, would accept that an inflation is accompanied by and arguably reinforced by, if not originally powered by, an increase in the money supply.

It has been all too often the fashion for competing schools of economists to haggle for a Government's soul, seeking to drive any Government to monotheism in its approach to inflation. In addition, the more vociferous and less scholarly of the proponents of any view attempt to castigate those who seek to find common ground, or who seek to criticise both parties in any dispute over a subject as complicated as inflation. This seems foolish in view of the genuine complexity of the problem before us. Any inflation is fuelled by rapid expansion of the money supply: in that sense we are all monetarists now. But the money supply may be expanding through the impact of high wage settlements on the public borrowing requirement, which in its turn will fuel further inflation. Excessive demand in relation to supply inevitably causes inflation in labour and product markets as firms bid for available resources, whilst monopolists and suppliers in turn exploit any market conditions which may arise that permit them to add cost-push elements to the system. Any exponent of the inflationary process has to look at velocities, at confidence and expectations, as well as at demand and the money aggregates that underlie that effective demand.

Whilst there are many relevant questions for a scholarly economist, there are only two major questions of relevance for a future Government. The first is how an accelerating inflation can be checked, if that is the situation which confronts the incoming politicians. The second is how are inflationary forces to be avoided, if a new Government is in the position of needing to stimulate a depressed economy with a high level of unemployment and other underutilised resources.

The answer to the first question hinges on the level of inflation prevailing, and the main instruments of its growth. At a very high level of inflation a dramatic act like the issue of a completely new currency may be necessary, along with a necessary package of measures to control government expenditure and the future money supply growth rate. At a lower rate of inflation, induced by growing inflationary expectations among the work force, a breathing space may have to be created by a statutory wages policy in the absence of any voluntary agreement. In both cases the Government and nationalised industries not only have to make it clear that they do not intend to finance an ever more rapid rate of inflation through their pay and money policies, but they also have to be willing to implement the policy in full in their own areas of activity.

Inflationary pressures are generated both internally and externally.

Broadly speaking those that are internal reflect domestic wage rates and the effect on domestic wage demands flowing from higher wage costs pushing up prices. It is possible for higher prices to reflect higher profit margins and greater corporate profitability. This cause is commonly argued by the unions as being a regular contributor to high price inflation in the United Kingdom; but the theory does not stand up to the evidence, which shows that the secular trend of profits as a percentage of gross national product has been declining for the last two decades. Profits (i.e. gross trading profits less stock appreciation) as a percentage of GNP fell from 14.6 per cent in 1963 to 8.5 per cent in 1973 and have fallen further subsequently [*Annual Abstract of Statistics*, 1974]. The return on capital employed in the United Kingdom has fallen from 13.9 per cent in 1955 to 8.4 per cent in 1973 [*Economic Trends*, November 1974, xl–xli]. Those pressures that are external reflect world inflation rates, and particularly the gyrations of world commodity markets. These external prices are also affected by the relative movements of export and import prices, the terms of trade, and the movement in currency markets. Pure monetarists argue that external forces are irrelevant, as there is an exchange mechanism, and if prices of imports rise a decision has to be made to buy fewer of them. However, the price elasticity of demand is not always sufficient to allow compensatory volume adjustment, and international currency management also interferes with free market forces.

Any counter-inflation strategy, whether intending to reduce inflation from a high rate, or trying to prevent its recurrence on a grand scale, has to consider these external problems. The commodity markets are essential to a country like the United Kingdom, heavily dependent on world trade. It has to be the aim of the EEC negotiators backed by British Ministers and MPs to secure stable contract arrangements for EEC commodity imports. We should also seek to use EEC bargaining power in a united effort over heavy crude oil prices, just as individual companies and importers should aim to reduce their dependence for supplies on highly volatile marginal commodity markets by entering into long-term contractual arrangements. It is also important on an EEC scale that every effort is made to reduce dependence on outside sources for commodities, this being possible in the case of food if not of fuel. The United Kingdom has one great advantage in the commodity struggle in having considerable reserves of oil, gas and coal as well as access to the European food suppliers. These advantages must be used to the full, in combating the problems created by the vociferous and successful political demands of certain basic-commodity-producing countries to a greater share of the world's wealth and resources at the expense of the industrialised West.

The terms of trade hinge upon relative rates of home and world inflation, and the success achieved in the commodity price strategy. It is important that the pound sterling is strengthened by reducing foreign borrowings currently financing part of the huge public sector deficit, and that the internal rate of inflation is curbed to stop further deterioration of sterling against the index of other major currencies. Stabilisation of the pound then reduces inflationary pressures caused by the sinking exchange rate.

Internal inflation requires something in the nature of a confidence trick to lower expectations, backed up by a firm policy on public expenditure. It is a political judgement whether a full statutory incomes policy is necessary, whether voluntary agreement is feasible, or whether a strong lead in the public sector by individual industries and departments would be possible and sufficient to lower the general level of wage settlements. The main problem in combating inflation lies in the public sector where there has traditionally been no reduction in employment following large wage increases, and where a new approach to employment levels and remuneration is needed. It is essential, however, that whichever course is chosen it is adhered to, and money is not printed to get the Government off the hook. It is not sufficient to curb the money supply, because curbing the money supply means a range of other policies centred upon reducing government expenditure which amount to lowering the rate of wage inflation.

In the case of evolving a strategy to reflate, after a terrifying round of inflation has been cured by a vicious deflation, similar considerations apply. First, public expenditure during a reflation must be controlled in cash terms, and not allowed to escalate on the assumption that cash flow is irrelevant to the public sector because of its borrowing powers. Secondly, in conjunction with this control must come a phased increase in the money supply such that capacity utilisation and output have a chance of responding to it, rather than a rapid increase leading primarily to increased prices all round. Thirdly, the public sector should exercise care in its levels of recruitment and the rates of remuneration offered.

The main temptation of any Government is to reflate too rapidly, and to reflate on more than one occasion, as the lags always bring the efficacy of the early reflationary moves into doubt. The major problem has always been that reflation takes the economy to an overheated position, without allowing time for confidence to build up, or without allowing the opportunity for capacity to be increased significantly to prevent over-heating resulting from a particular package or packages of reflationary measures. The speed of reflations and their ephemeral nature has restricted investment and therefore limited the opportunities for major productivity gains. At the top of a boom in uncontrolled conditions Government expenditure and borrowing become too large, the balance of payments deteriorates rapidly as imports of primary and finished products are sucked in, and interest rates rise. In controlled conditions profitability falls through price restraint, adding a further disincentive to investment, whilst the public sector is denuded of labour as the private sector finds ways around wage and salary controls.

It is this debilitating cycle of accentuated stop-go that we have to tackle. There are two major ways of tackling it. The first is monetary and fiscal gradualism combined with policies to encourage high productivity. The second is the idea of regulating the relationship between our own cycle and that of the world economy.

Trade cycles have always been a feature of economic life, and the second half of the twentieth century has achieved some progress in halving the average length of the cycle. The position of the UK economy is particularly subject to world market pressures. Our economy is sensitive to world markets because we need such a wide range of imports, both to feed and clothe ourselves, and as raw materials for our industrial production. The 1972—4 boom was accentuated because most of the major Western economies, including the UK, were moving in concert. When we needed greater quantities of wool, cotton, oil, food, metals and timber, so did the rest of the world. Prices consequently accelerated rapidly. Similarly, when we were trying to correct our balance of payments deficit in 1974—5, the task was made more difficult by the international recession which meant a low level of demand for our exports.

As a result of chance factors delaying the UK recession in 1974, mainly reflecting government demand management whilst playing the electoral cycle, we now have an opportunity of moving a little out of phase with the world economy. This would permit us to export to booming economies whilst we are still operating at a modest level of domestic demand, and then to import more cheaply and export through better terms of trade in the go part of our cycle. This expedient could remove the worst external pressures from the domestic economy.

The major constraint, however, still remains the long-term rate of growth. The comparatively low level of productivity and the low rate of increase in productivity in the UK economy has for years been the major constraint on our economic performance. Government has to devote its energies to tackling the problems which are reflected in this situation.

Firstly, there are the structural imbalances in the economy. The UK has never managed to evolve a satisfactory policy towards declining industries: the difficulties in the cotton and shipbuilding industries in the 1930s are paralleled in the coal industry in the 1960s and the mass-market car industry in the 1970s. The problem has been one of a lack of mobility of labour, and a wish on the part of governments to bolster existing employment structures rather than encourage the development of new industries to absorb the resources being shed by the declining sectors. An integral part of this process must be full consultation with the work forces concerned, the provision of retraining facilities, help with removal expenses, and other incentives to encourage redeployment. The basic aim of policy should be to spend government money on helping mobility, and on supporting new developing industries, rather than spending money on fossilising the industrial structure and encouraging immobility through large council house subsidies, indiscriminate help to ailing industries like the mass-production car industry, and other similar disincentive policies. Particularly important is the provision of facilities to give people new skills and the confidence needed to change their jobs and move on.

Secondly, there are the resource imbalances created by such a large public sector, which demands ever larger revenue subsidies, and which raises capital investment money without having to pass any market test for that investment. Restoration of financial independence to communications, transport and energy industries would make both an immediate contribution to limiting public expenditure and controlling the money supply, and to correcting resource misallocations.

The restoration of financial independence should act as a stimulus to efficiency in the nationalised sector. The UK nationalised industries have an appalling record, with lower productivity per man than any comparable Western European or Japanese undertaking, and a very poor return on capital employed. Both these defects must be remedied by new capital investment, proper pricing policies, and an attack upon overmanning through natural wastage. There is a good argument for not employing a single new person in any nationalised industry for a period of two years. If this tactic were adopted there would be no need to make anyone redundant, whilst switching between departments and industries could avoid the worst effects of imbalance caused by differential rates of wastage between different types of employee. An improvement in public sector efficiency would have a beneficial effect on productivity in the economy as a whole in view of the size of the nationalised industries in the economy.

The problem of unemployment is the most challenging problem which the United Kingdom economy faces. There are commentators who, rightly perceiving the ills of inflation, regard rising unemployment as a desirable policy to cure this ill. To do so is to substitute one intractable social problem for another, and to substitute one which is arguably worse than the disease which it attempts to cure. Unemployment means hardship for people who are genuinely seeking work, and who are unable to find any. It means a waste of talent and energy in our society. It encourages despondency and despair. Unemployment of any resource — above all of labour — adversely affects the standards of life of the whole of society and not only those of the unemployed. Post-war politicians have correctly attempted to adhere to a policy of near full employment; it is essential that government remains wedded to this notion. The worrying features of the cycles between 1972 and 1976 have been on the one hand the accelerating level of government deficits, and on the other hand the intolerable levels of unemployment created deliberately to cure the consequent inflation.

Attacking the cancer of inflation through a more adequate money supply policy and through care in pursuing any reflationary ambitions is the first step in dealing with the problem of unemployment. The second important step lies in fostering policies which help raise the rate of productivity, and lead to the generation of more consumable income and wealth within our society. Inflation visibly prices people out of jobs. The last cycle has made this abundantly clear: you need only to look at the falling volume effects on the business of the Post Office resulting from the 67 per cent increase in telephone charges in the autumn of 1976, and from the increase in postage rates of over 600 per cent in the period from 1969 to 1976. In 1975 alone, the average phone call doubled in price, and the average letter post went up by 87 per cent. Increased prices resulting from higher wage settlements in a labour-intensive industry dissuaded people from using the service as they otherwise would have done, and inevitably led to the need for labour-shedding and work-sharing in an industry which with a lower pricing policy would undoubtedly have provided more activity and therefore more wealth and income for everyone involved.

It is often objected that financial independence of the nationalised industries entails labour-shedding, that control of the money supply and government expenditure is deflationary, and that a harsher attitude towards declining industries also tends to greater unemployment. There is sufficient truth in all of these propositions to warrant analysis, but like so many politically oriented statements they amount to little more than half-truths. Financial independence of the nationalised industries should entail a more positive attitude towards the development of new markets, new services and products, which can employ the existing labour force in more productive activities, which can generate more income and more profit for society at large. It is the fabric of price control, of large wage increases within the context of a sluggish strategy towards markets and products, that has led to the financial crisis in the nationalised industries which besets us today. Control of the money supply and of government expenditure is not necessarily deflationary. It is a policy which attempts to influence the balance of resources between public and private, and also attempts to ensure that resources are used in the most efficient and productive way. This cannot be deflationary: it can prevent inflation, and as a sensibly pursued package of policies it can ensure a higher rate of growth in the economy as a whole, which will entail more income and wealth for everyone.

One must concede that a harsher attitude towards declining industries is also a policy which may in the short term produce hardship in that people who have been employed in an industry most of their life or all of their life may find that that industry can no longer support them in their occupation. Given sensible policies for early retirement the worst social consequences of allowing the rundown of unproductive and outmoded industries can be overcome, and the economy as a whole can benefit by retraining people for more productive uses in which they will make a greater contribution to the wealth and prosperity of the whole nation. Government must take every opportunity to foster and support compensatory employment opportunities through creating the right atmosphere in which business can operate, and supporting training programmes within the economy. The broad areas in which employment should increase ought to lie in export industries and services, service activities for the home market, high technology and specialised manufacturing sectors, and new product and growth areas like plastics, pharmaceuticals and chemicals. The strategy of the counter-cyclical economy combined with a lower rate of domestic inflation should lead to a shift of resources into exports: in this connection the opportunities for selling management and professional expertise in growth areas in the Middle East, South America and parts of Africa are of great importance.

A strategy of setting industry free, of rewarding entrepreneurship and initiative, of reducing high taxation rates on corporations and individuals alike and marking proper limits to the public deployment of resources could give every incentive to create a better balanced economy, a more invigorating atmosphere to replace the museum economy philosophy which now confronts us. At the moment it seems to be the intention of policy makers to take the existing employment structure as being the ideal one for the economy, and to freeze it at whatever price in subsidisation and call on government resources this might entail. In place of the archival preservation of dead or dying industries we need to put belief in ourselves to create employment, to make products and provide services which the world at large wishes to buy, and which can improve our own standards of life at home. We have now seen that a policy of indiscriminate government subsidisation and expenditure leads to inflation, which in its turn leads to a harsh reality of dole queues, despair and frenetic self-questioning. The people of our country are able and well educated, not the material for the dole queue, the declining industry, or the lack of prospects which confront so many of our ablest people through no particular fault of their own. It must be the task of an incoming Government to set the people free, to congratulate the profit makers rather than to tax them and legislate against them, to congratulate those who invest and accumulate and save in order to provide the British economy with the machine power which it requires to compete with the Japanese, the Americans and the Germans. The country which pioneered the first industrial revolution, now needs another revolution in attitude and in the role of government in order to bring its economy back to the first division in the league rather than letting it continue to sink into the mire of economic failure.

The UK economy is a declining economy relative to world output, but it is an internationally oriented economy where we have to plan in an international context. First, commodity producers' power does necessitate home resource control over utilisation. Secondly, developing countries are going to want to control part of the industries growing up in their economies, and the role of the Western nations is a participatory and advisory one rather than ownership. Thirdly, our comparative advantage lies not in mass-produced goods, but in specialist and high-technology goods, and in services. To sustain these advantages the economy must maintain a high standard of education, and must foster initiative and enterprise.

The argument of this chapter has not centred upon the dismantling of the welfare state, or on the reduction of the high environmental and welfare standards that we have rightly come to expect. The main contention, that government expenditure and the growth of the public sector have to be arrested, is an argument over the control and management of services and industry. Welfare benefits, a health and education service and other transfer benefits are and must remain an integral part of our society.

It is rather the contention of this chapter that more resources can be freed for higher standards of health and welfare service, by curbing the scope of public sector industrial activity, and curbing the marginal services and activities that have proliferated in government. The ending of nationalised industry revenue subsidies and allocating housing and food subsidies to individuals rather than indiscriminately would reduce public expenditure by 10 per cent, whilst Government should, through its fiscal and industrial policies, encourage profitability and new ventures, rather than seek to fossilise the economy by subsidies. The prime aim of our strategy must be to raise the long-term rate of growth, thus generating more wealth and income in order to afford better private and public standards.

The dangers in our current economic position are obvious. Hyper-inflation cannot be ruled out if reflation is handled clumsily. Deep recession is to many economists the only way of curbing inflation. Both these phenomena are damaging to society as a whole. Our balance of payments remains weak at any reasonable level of activity, and our rate of growth is sluggish in comparison with our expectations. To break out of this wearisome cycle of problems we need to reverse our policy of an uncontrolled public sector and a declining and squeezed private sector. We need to reward enterprise, to lower taxes and to foster choice and competition, investment and growth. To do this we have to reverse the trend towards private squalor and public excesses, reverse the notion that the public purse is bottomless and that credit flows eternal. Above all we need to believe in ourselves, and build on the skills and abilities of our people, which remain our most important resource.

7 Housing and Society

JOHN PATTEN

Amongst the many manifestations of a country in economic distress that are evident in the United Kingdom in the mid-1970s is its housing crisis. There are apparently not enough 'roofs-over-heads' and thus there is homelessness. There are, in addition, anything between two and four million 'unfit' houses that do not come up to acceptable standards: this is because we have probably the oldest housing stock in Europe, an at present outdated holding of dwellings that is ever-increasing in size despite – often unwise – efforts expended on clearance and rebuilding, and – more recently and more wisely – on rehabilitation. The crisis exists on the one hand because finance for home ownership is becoming available to fewer people and then only at a higher cost, and on the other because finance for publicly owned homes is not only equally hard to come by from hard-pressed local and national resources, but also because it is in a chaotic form, seemingly unrelated to the economic realities of a properly conducted subsidised system. There is certainly a crisis because people's rightful and reasonable expectations of better housing are not being met: this is a fact that is exacerbated by the contemporary trend towards younger marriages, earlier break-up of different generations of families that once might have lived for a while under the same roof, and the desire for second homes by the more affluent. Equally there exists a crisis because inadequate housing brings with it such deep social problems among young and adults alike that not only does it cause personal distress and a lot of public expenditure on the part of the social services in trying to solve the resultant problems, but it may attack the very roots and stability of our society.

The crisis exists despite the central paradox of Britain's housing situation, that nationally there is a crude surplus of homes over households over half a million existing next to homelessness. Also, between three and four million people are badly housed, a dreadful fact. The most fundamental way of looking at our housing problem is thus not as 'roofs-over-heads', but as basic to our overall social policy. Housing is at the core of any social policy. It is not just something on the road to sturdy economic independence, for from good housing much else follows. We must freely admit that there is something wrong with a British society which has under-occupation and a surplus of some types of housing and yet homelessness; that provides what is in theory a comprehensive range of social services and yet throws up bad homes and problem families, as Ann Spokes points out in the next chapter. The security and confidence of a home is a very important factor in the normal functioning of family life, conditioning children as they grow up in their role in society.

Thus, any comprehensive housing philosophy must start off from a clear assessment of need and not from any party dogma. It must recognise the historical background to, and historical inertia of, most housing situations and the geographical variation that exists in them — for needs, and therefore potential solutions, vary regionally, and between town and country.

The dimensions and characteristics of the present housing situation really date only from the time of the First World War. Before the beginning of the century the majority of housing in England was neither owner-occupied nor publicly owned. Despite the efforts of Disraeli's reforming ministries, and the Acts that his Home Secretary, Cross, had introduced to improve sanitation and the conditions of artisans' and labourers' dwellings, there had been no major extensions of home ownership. Yet on the other hand true public — or 'social', as I prefer to call it — housing had barely come into being. It was the age not of the housing authority, but of the charitable trusts, the Peabodys and Guinnesses, and of the enlightened builders of Bournville or Saltaire. The majority of houses, over three-quarters, were privately rented; by the end of the nineteenth century house building had approached the not unhealthy rate for then of 150,000 units a year, but largely built for rent. This was the peak, however, of that form of tenure.

The rise in home ownership, and in social housing, both date from then. Social housing gathered momentum with the desire to build homes for returning heroes in 1919. Council housing was used as the weapon to house those who could not house themselves. Since then some six million council houses or other units have been built; they have undoubtedly not only put that many more roofs over far more heads, but made a great contribution to the social stability of the country and to personal and family well-being. The popular contention that council estates are always drab or vandal-torn is grossly misleading. And we must remember that in their construction Tory Governments have been, to a considerable measure, interventionist, for example in the subsidy arrangements of the 1920s and 1930s. Equally, some Tory-controlled local authorities have built them with zest at some times and sold them at others. Harold Macmillan in his great housing drive of the early 1950s used local authorities as his agents. It must be clearly seen, however, that council housing has never fulfilled all the needs that private landlords were attempting, and failing, to fulfil before the 1914 war. To quote the author of one most influential and important recent book on housing in regard to council provision,

> The contribution to human happiness over the past fifty years must have been enormous, and for all their shortcomings has left a legacy of immense value to the coming generation. *And yet, as a solution of the basic housing problems facing this country, council housing must be deemed a failure.* [Fred Berry, *Housing: the Great British Failure* (Charles Knight, 1974): italics mine.]

It will never succeed in relation to a problem which, as supporters of increasing the proportion of home ownership must also not allow themselves to forget, is getting worse — i.e. there is now more homelessness, not less, despite an apparent greater affluence and much greater government expenditure in recent years. The home-ownership movement must take its share of blame for this, as must its political proponents.

The ramifications of the problem as posed do not stop with the historical legacy of a problem that has developed its exact present-day style in the post-1919 era. Basic geographical and regional facts must also be borne in mind; they are still too often ignored. There is no doubt that there is considerable regional variation in types and levels of housing provision. It is difficult for people at the margins of getting a mortgage to buy a house in or near central London. Yet the same income can easily purchase one in north Norfolk or Lincolnshire, though regional inequalities in income levels must be taken into account. Equally, in some parts of the West Country it is, if not actually easy, at least easier to get a council house than in areas of acute housing stress like Lambeth, or those places where building land is severely restricted by Green Belt and physical constraints, as in the case of a city like Oxford. Freedom of choice and ability to move house, for a third example, are much more strictly limited for council house tenants than for the home-owner. Different local authorities have different policies as far as this is concerned, just as the heritage of the last fifty years or so has led them to vary enormously in their provision of social housing. In addition then to more houses built, we need more fine-tuning of our housing provision, social and private, to meet the problems that the varied history of the past fifty years has left us with and to meet considerable regional and rural/urban variations that exist.

Any comprehensive approach, recognising the legacy of the past, and its strong regional variations, must live with our ageing housing stock. It is the framework within which our housing policy until the end of the century and beyond must be viewed. It must also be based on a clear assessment of need. Too often both these facts have been ignored. To take our ageing housing stock first, a great deal is rightly made of housing starts and completions each year, but the fact remains that even in a good year not more than about 2 per cent is added to the nation's housing stock; at present the annual increase in stock amounts to only 1½ per cent of the total existing stock (1975 figures). Since any country's housing stock, in a time of great economic difficulty, cannot easily be expanded, it is clearly no more than prudent to make the best use of houses that we can, by keeping them in good repair and, of course, improving them from time to time as rising standards and expectations dictate. Not only this, but we must also constantly explore ways of stretching housing stock, to make it *go* further.

Taking into account present-day rates of clearance and building, two out of every three houses that are going to be in existence in the year 2000 are already up. Well over a third of our present-day stock was built before 1914, and perhaps four in every ten of Britain's houses, if not indeed slums or in need of decent sanitary facilities or unfit, are at least inadequate — inadequate in the sense that they are poorly heated or have little or no storage space, or above all are very cramped, though they may be 'fit' by present public health standards. Yet in many countries sixty years or less is considered a decent lifetime for a house. This takes us back to the eve of the First World War, a watershed in many ways in standards of housing provision in England. Purely theoretically, at current rates of clearance — even if it is ever economically viable or environmentally and socially desirable to clear on any scale — perhaps not even two million dwellings could be replaced by the year 2000. And we now more clearly realise that the bulldozer is not a universal panacea. Housing problems are not solved by driving bulldozers at them, any more than social problems can be solved by having money thrown at them. But by the year 2000 another four million dwellings will have reached the same age, though many of these of course will have been better built, in the 1920s and 1930s, with their higher standards.

Indeed, just as construction is constrained, and rightly, by Green Belts, by tighter planning laws and by a whole new planning philosophy that is against comprehensive redevelopment on social grounds, so people's attitudes to their built environment have totally changed. Public opinion more and more has set its face against the wanton destruction of older buildings as well, of course, as the older living communities that they house. The fact is that politicians have not woken up to the reality of living with an ageing housing stock with all the economic, social and political implications that this contains. We are going to have to live, it may be concluded, with rehabilitation and re-use as a fact of economic, of environmental, of social, and therefore of political life.

Equally, local and national politicians do not always seem to have clearly assessed actual need for housing in terms of different types of provision. The wrong sorts of houses may be being built, sometimes in the wrong places. In this, councils seem to be the main offenders, though the private sector cannot be entirely absolved from blame. There are, *Social Trends for 1974* tells us, |19·890 million dwellings in the United Kingdom — 52 per cent owner-occupied, 31 per cent rented from local authorities and 17 per cent from private owners, together with trusts and housing associations, etc. Within this total, the most immediate trend is the ever-increasing numbers of small households. By 1971, 49.3 per cent of all households in the United Kingdom (of which there are 18.18 million) consisted of one or two persons. In 1961, one-person households were about 12 per cent of the whole; by 1971 18 per cent. In 1961, two-person households were 22 per cent of the whole and by 1971 had reached 31 per cent. The need for the single-person and two-person unit is considerable. Yet it is one housing problem that is still given relatively little attention. Clear policy on it has been non-existent for all practical purposes until recently, and is far from clear today.

In particular, public sector policy in housebuilding, despite some notable exceptions, is still too often concerned with the blanket construction of family units, together with sheltered housing for the aged. Yet trends at work in society today positively demand greater attention to this problem. For example, taking the crowded and urbanised south-east, where need for this sort of housing provision may be thought to be high, figures provided in the recent report of the National Economic Development Office suggest that by far the greatest growth in private households between mid-1969 and mid-1981 will be in the one-person household. Married-couple-with-children households, the classic type whose needs the housing policy of all parties seems designed to try to satisfy, are estimated to be going to grow by about 7 per cent overall in this period. Yet by comparison one-person households will grow by three times as much, over 20 per cent. We must develop a housing philosophy that clearly recognises needs such as this, rather than reflecting bureaucratic habits as its base.

To date, council housing has failed to reach those most in need. It did not, for example, until relatively recently, really cater properly for the elderly — not only to their disadvantage, but to the disadvantage of the whole of society in need of housing. It is disagreeable for old people to live alone in two- or three-bedroom council houses, with loneliness, the danger of hypothermia from inability to pay for adequate heating in a house of that size, consequent drain on social and domiciliary services, etc. It would be agreeable for them to be better housed, in smaller units, be they one-bedroom flats, two-bedroom bungalows, in groups or by themselves and with or without attendant wardens. Though segregation and distinction by age is surely not what most retired people want, the 'Granny Flat' is better than the retired folks' ghetto. But, whatever solutions are applied, it is a shameful blot on our society that many old people suffer from any or all of five of what the community physician, Dr Muir Grey, has called the 'Dis-eases'. These are Poverty; Isolation; Bad Housing; Being Cold; and the Inability to be Independent. When these are overlapped, as they often are, by the consequence of being handicapped, the situation is even less desirable for the old: some two-thirds of our disabled people are over sixty-five years of age. Most old – or any other – people, don't usually want to leave the community in which their house and life is embedded. Shops, neighbours, pubs, churches, may well be more attractive forces than the actual bricks and mortar of the family home. Individual units to move to are more alluring a prospect than institutions. It must be recognised that the whole country's housing problems are bound up in part with the problems of elderly people, stemming mainly from a failure to build small dwellings in the past forty years. This is despite the fact that now about a third of all local authority housing starts are for the elderly.

A building programme which allowed them to move house within the same area would be of great advantage to them as individuals and to the community at large. Homes that are under-occupied would be freed from the community. Under-occupation of council and privately owned houses cannot fail to increase owing to the excess of the family house, predominately three-bedroomed, until well into the 1960s. There are many estates built before then, and some after, which consist mainly of family houses from which the children are beginning to leave. These are the under-occupied estates of the very near future, which have little room for building of small units to provide a better mix: though conversion of some traditional three-bedroomed houses could give a 'Granny Flat' on the ground floor and a similar unit for the young marrieds or able single person on the first floor. The lack of a clear housing policy for the elderly serves as one example of how genuinely needs-orientated housing policies have not been developed, and sets the scene for an examination of the three main sectors of British housing today – the privately rented and voluntary sector; the social sector; and the home-owned sector.

The privately rented sector is beating the retreat. Between 1961 and 1971 the stock of dwellings to rent decreased from 5.2 million to 3.7 million: unfurnished lettings have almost vanished: and the supply of furnished lettings is drying up as a result of the 1974 Rent Act, on top of previous legislation. This Act represents one more blow, perhaps the final body blow, in government attacks and controls on the rented sector. As we have seen, before 1914 something over three-quarters of the dwellings in the country were privately owned, and let out to tenants. The picture has changed radically today. That is not to say that governments have not, from time to time, tried to encourage private renting, whether by the modification of rent control as in 1957 or 1965, or by government subsidies to private tenants, as in 1972. Yet now only 12 per cent of our dwellings are privately rented, and the decline is likely to continue. They are on their way out, with disastrous effects on the housing prospects for the homeless or near-homeless, who are faced with the council house waiting list and perhaps the council-provided bed-and-breakfast; for the mobile young, who need this kind of short-term accommodation; and for students in our colleges, polytechnics and universities, few of which can house all their students, a situation likely to be exacerbated by cutbacks on capital building projects. Because of this Act there has developed a macabre auction between students, the young and the poor and the socially disadvantaged, for what remains.

I do not believe a needs-orientated policy – as opposed to a doctrinally based policy – could have produced the 1974 Rent Act legislation, and it is worth while demonstrating why this is the case. It represents a serious curtailment of free housing choice, and a threat to the supply of housing in the private rented sector in London and other major cities, where the problems of homelessness are most acute. Resident landlords, even taking into account that the Act gives them exemption from security of tenure, will be overshadowed by the fear that a future Government could give security of tenure even to lodgers in the landlord's own home. A huge measure of uncertainty has been introduced; how can landlords in this climate be expected to open their homes to tenants?

Certainly the Act has helped pull up the ladder on the homeless in our cities, and increased under-occupation rates in our housing stock which is working at under-capacity. As the Francis Committee, appointed to examine the rented sector by the 1966–70 administration, wrote with some foresight, 'Greater security for those in occupation when the extended security code came into force could well be bought at the cost of greater hardship and difficulty for the much larger number of households seeking such accommodation.' It really is doubtful whether established tenants will reap any appreciable extra benefit to measure against the great disadvantage to would-be tenants with no other outlets. The cost far outweights the benefit. There is no *need* to make it impossible for landlord and tenant to enter into a clearly defined legal agreement, and indeed the making of this practically, if not explicitly, impossible is a clearcut trespass on individual freedom. In the interests of these, and of other more mobile, transient households which are at present dependent on private furnished accommodation, it is vital to free constraints on what remains of the privately rented sector; always safeguarding, of course, benefits of tenure conferred up to and including the 1974 Act. A whole variety of short leases and shortholds could be devised to fit given situations. This would be not only expedient and practical, but socially just to all parties involved.

Such a course of action would not solve a great proportion of our housing problems all over the country, but it would undoubtedly satisfy some of the demand for this sort of housing felt primarily in our crowded inner cities. The privately rented sector does not, however, stop with the private landlord *strictu sensu*. The role of the charitable trusts, of course, was once considerable, particularly in alleviating some urban housing problems in the days before social housing was provided. But the Guinness Trust and the rest can do little to expand their role today. The 'third arm' of the housing movement has, instead, developed into the housing association, housing society, co-ownership schemes and the rest, a half-world between renting and ownership in which the Housing Corporation now plays a major part. In its early days the Corporation encouraged the provision of housing which catered for a particular section of the community, but this has now changed and its future field of operation is much wider, particularly in areas of economic stress. It now seems to be encouraging housing association operations in areas of rehabilitation. It could, and should, be used more and more in the field of voluntary and self-help housing. There is no reason, for example, why it should not help the student unions of colleges and polytechnics provide student co-operative dwellings and students' housing associations. At least ten times as much is now spent on student housing than in 1964 yet the situation grows worse. This has serious implications for the stability of society as have other sorts of poor housing provision. Students, like any other part of society, are going to be fundamentally discontented if they are inadequately housed. At best they may work badly and be emotionally disoriented: at worst they may be prey to the pressures of extreme political groups of whatever complexion. Better planning for their housing must be introduced. The role of the Housing Corporation in encouraging a great variety of housing associations is potentially great, maintaining and indeed widening freedom of choice.

In contrast to private and other forms of rented accommodation, the public, or social, sector has been growing steadily since the end of the First World War. This has usually been by construction. But, particularly under the present administration, the process of 'municipalisation' of previously privately owned accommodation has led to the addition of a heterogeneous collection of houses and flats to the municipal stock. Such purchases, of course, do not increase the total stock of housing, but merely mark a change in form of ownership and tenure. There is no doubt at all that there will always have to be publicly owned housing to let, and rightly so. There will always be those who are unable to afford and/or manage their own home, or those who do not wish to do so. Indeed, the acceptance of freedom of choice as a principle would seem to dictate that some council housing must always be available, as should that owned by private landlords or by housing associations for rent. Certainly only the most extremely doctrinaire would wish to see the frontiers of social housing rolled back completely or, on the other hand, advanced to the limits.

Social housing is here to stay. But that fact does not, and should not, prevent one asking questions about it, and its nature. For example, is the fact that over 30 per cent of Britain's housing is in public ownership a matter for congratulation or concern? Is that proportion right? Should it be extended or reduced? Is social housing the *right* way to spend often scarce resources? Is social housing socially desirable? But in enquiring we must recognise that Britain has a more humane and generous approach to housing than many other, ostensibly richer, societies. The debate between those who regard social housing as an universalistic social service or a residual provision is not easily resolved in this light.

The contribution to human happiness provided by council housing has been vast: it has also been vastly expensive. 'Has the expenditure been worth while?' is the first question. Should more have been spent, or in different ways? Could the same money have bought more happiness? By the end of the financial year 1975/76 the accumulated loan debt on social housing expenditure — some of it going back more than half a century — will have reached between £16,000 and £17,000 million. This has doubled in the last five years, and it is equivalent to a third of the National Debt. It has given people both roofs-over-heads in the structural sense, and homes in a social and a psychological sense. In the structural sense many council tenants may be better off than some owner-occupiers. A tenant in a socially owned house — whether in the high-density, high-rise city blocks or in the single family houses of the new and expanding towns — is quite privileged. Not only because of the fact that, as Richard Crossman once rather surprisingly described them, council tenants are 'a cossetted and privileged clan in our society . . . because a council house is a prize hard to come by', but because his or her home, after the prize is won, and especially if it was built after the mid-1960s, is likely to have standards of size and fittings now rare in the cheaper privately built house. Council tenants also have complete security of tenure, if they continue to pay their rents and rates. Perhaps they should have more than this. It is scarcely necessary to invoke psychological and economic benefits to explain the general trend toward owner-occupation that has outpaced social ownership from roughly the same starting-point, despite high interest rates and rising prices. The benefits of full or part home-ownership include some things which social housing tenants have — like security of tenure, yet others which they do not have. They do not have freedom from interference, and they do not have the freedom and incentive to modify, maintain and improve their homes. Neither do they have the capital-accumulating benefits of ownership.

Social housing has often led to rising frustrations for tenants unable even to paint their own front door a chosen colour, on the one hand, and for housing authorities from rising costs of maintenance, on the other. I do not wish here to go into the details of council house finance, capital costs or running expenditure. But the success or failure of council housing must be judged on financial as well as human grounds, and the numbers and sorts of homes provided weighed against cost and alternatives. The cost of Britain's social housing is now rising so fast that, as some experts admit, it is already threatening to disrupt the entire structure of local government finance, and the mechanisms of government support for it. By the 1980s, if present trends continue, the accumulated public housing debt will have risen to some £30,000 million. The annual interest charges on this alone could wipe out the whole of the Government's expected revenue from North Sea oil at peak production. About 60 per cent of local government debt is financed for less than five years. In today's economic circumstances, the terms and cost of refinancing debts, and of raising new loans, is bound to have a very serious effect upon the whole public sector deficit. So are maintenance charges, whilst the proportion that council tenants actually contribute has fallen from about 75 per cent in 1968 to about 43 per cent in 1975, and this last figure takes into account the enormous subsidy represented by rent rebates of over £200 million per annum.

The percentage of household income spent on rent by council tenants was, in late 1975, less than 10 per cent; a figure in real terms in England and Wales, allowing for rebates, of just £2.85! This scarcely seems socially just. It is correct and proper that those who can pay no more than this should not have to do so, but why should families with a combined income of £100 a week and more pay rents of much less than £10 a week? In 1974 about 80 per cent of council tenants had gross household incomes of less than £4000 per annum, and less than 1 per cent had incomes over £8000. Yet there remained a substantial proportion of nearly 20 per cent who had incomes between £4000 and £8000 per annum who could, and in the name of social justice should, pay more. The electoral sensitivity of the issue is such that council housing has been raised to the status of a sacred cow, and it seems inevitable that for years ahead, unless the political will is produced, major housing policy decisions will continue to be made with little reference to any financial or social reality. Millions and millions of pounds have been and are being spent on council houses and needless municipalisation, yet the housing lists grow longer, not shorter; and the shameful blot on our society of tens of thousands homeless, and hundreds of thousands badly housed, remains.

We must brace ourselves to ask the seemingly blasphemous question (at least to Socialists): 'How fair is this system?' Is it fair to the country's finances? The answer is no. Is it fair to allocate subsidies to many who do not need them in quite such an over-generous way? The answer again is no. Social housing should be based on need, not on demand as is the case with the National Health Service and certain of the social services. Less than a third of the country's people enjoy the facility of a socially owned house, and many of them have been allocated these without real reference to real need. Rational analysis must prevail over what Messrs Booker and Grey [in the *Observer*, 11 May 1975] called 'the quasi-religious mystification of Labour housing policy' — rational analysis which is being made increasingly difficult by the drying-up of the privately rented sector, the only one which has received virtually no subsidy, and by the widely predicted effect of the Community Land Act which, it seems, may gradually dry up much of the supply of land for housing. Booker and Grey, hardly perhaps the most noted supporters of the Conservative Party in the country, conclude in the same article that the Labour Government has made the housing situation far worse:

> ... by dispensing with the albeit moderate disciplines of the Tory Housing Finance Act, while at the same time allowing unwise capital expenditure to burgeon, it has ensured that in the months and years to come more money will be spent on less housing than ever before – while what little housing is produced will do little to alleviate the problems of those who most need help.

What can be done? Let us look first of all at rents, and at standards of new construction. Asking tenants who are able to do so to pay more rent seems perfectly reasonable, socially just, and economically useful. There is no question that tenants could ever pay the full economic cost of renting, or that such an approach would solve the chaotic state of social housing finance; but that is not to say that council house rents should be maintained at their scandalously low levels for all. As Fred Berry again has written,

> If householders are ready to spend more on food and clothing, never mind more expensive, less essential spending, and if they are to insist on higher wages, there is no justification for them to retain the rent levels of ten or twenty years ago if a rise would help the tenants of more recently built dwellings.

A revision of rents upwards to the percentage levels of 1968 under the previous Labour administration, when council house tenants provided about 75 per cent of the running costs of their houses, from today's absurdly low level of around 40 per cent would seem economically sound and socially just. Rent rebates are available for those who cannot pay; awful spectres of means tests are always raised at such suggestions, yet no great sympathy would be forthcoming for house purchasers if they complained at being, as they are, means-tested by housing societies. But even if this were to occur, capital costs would not be much helped. Building and purchase by councils on borrowed money costs much more than it used to do. Our present housing crisis has made it abundantly clear that we cannot build our way out of trouble by the social sector. Other means must be found on economic grounds alone; both major parties, in varying degrees, favour home-ownership. So do most people in this country, given the chance. Surely need, economic necessity and personal social choice can be met at the same time to a higher degree than at present. And municipalisation can be dismissed as a tool of any use to end homelessness in a sentence; for it fails to add one more unit to the overall national pool of housing. In almost every case it represents a clear misuse of money in short supply that should be spent on adding to the housing stock by new construction.

Certainly new construction should be freed of standards that, under present Parker-Morris conventions, seem over-rigorous compared with private building standards. These standards should be abolished forthwith, as they are one of the most serious inhibitors of speed and flexibility in housing construction. Local authorities would be better off with complete flexibility to design homes to meet their particular local requirements. If small units are to be experimented with, the Parker-Morris approach is clearly the wrong one. Planning procedures, too, should be speeded up; time costs money in housing. The Dobry Report (1975) has pointed the way. Much radical change is needed to improve their cost-effectiveness, though any speeding-up must be balanced by proper concern for conservation and environmental factors. And we also need more flexibility in conversion policies of councils to meet real *need*. More attention should be given to the possibility of conversions of existing single-family houses. In addition, under-occupation of council houses is a great waste of resources; it seems that too many authorities still place obstacles in the way of tenants taking in lodgers if they wish to do so. Equally mobility should be made easier between social housing in different parts of the country, and councils should positively encourage the taking in of lodgers on Rent Act terms as an important means of helping individuals and small homeless households, as well as transient workers and young people needing temporary lodgings. Why should the tenants of socially owned houses not be treated as responsible enough to manage lodgers, compared with home-owners? Too often, council estates still seem run on a neo-feudal system with exactly that measure of paternalism typical of the country landowner that was once the *bête noire* of Fabian Socialists at the turn of the century. Users of socially provided housing are, by and large, treated with as little concern for their individuality as broiler chickens in a battery farm. Rent books are there to remind them of their duties, but little of their reciprocal rights. They must keep no lodgers, no dogs, no pigeons; responsibility and freedom of choice are too often denied; this must surely be to the detriment, psychologically and socially, of council tenants. Frank Field, the (socialist) Director of the Child/Poverty Action Group, and of the Low Pay Unit, was indeed moved to describe council tenants in March 1976 as being treated like serfs.

Paternalism of this sort really was on the way out on country estates at the turn of the century. Indeed, over the whole range of the social services, broadly interpreted, there has been a major shift from benevolent philanthropy to the right of the individual as the basis of citizenship. The means test has been replaced by service-on-demand throughout the social services, though not in social housing – a paradoxical situation. In housing, the corollary that responsibility, as well as rights, must also pass from government to governed has simply been ignored. In housing, the failure to promote opportunities for the exercise of individual responsibility is compounded by the increasing lack of any alternative to the docile acceptance of a council tenancy. We need to look at ways of breaking up the uniformity which characterises the management of socially owned housing, as we must its forms of tenure. We need the transfer of more social responsibility to the tenants of socially owned houses as much as we need the transfer of part or full ownership to those that want it.

We need a tenants' statement of rights to make this possible. The idea should be part and parcel of Tory philosophy, in fact, embodying as a basic right for council tenants the rights of self-determination and maximum freedom of choice. There is a whole shopping-list of things a Tenants' Charter might contain. Certainly, every estate should have a properly formed and democratically elected tenants' association which local authorities should consult about the development, improvement and amenities of the estate. In time, such associations might well take over some of the responsibility for programmes of minor works or improvements, and might be given a budget by the local authorities. This would be not only socially desirable, but could well save on the running costs of houses, and certainly shorten the often ridiculously long waiting time for even minor repairs. I am quite sure that the more people can be involved in these matters the more they will feel responsible for the whole quality of life and their environment, and it would indeed be surprising if we did not see a welcome downturn in the vandalism that now goes on in certain areas. This is often directly a result of social problems, as it is of the inadequate provision of play areas, poor environmental design of estates, and suchlike.

The time has come to end the managerial feudalism of many council estates, and to give people the chance of more say, more involvement in, and thus, I believe, more commitment to the environment in which they live. Integral to this, of course, must be the positive right to choose ownership, or part ownership, or more varied forms of tenure like long leases. Anyone who has lived in a council house for a reasonable length of time, say three or four years, should have the absolute right to buy either the freehold, a share of the equity, or a long lease on the house or flat. The dead hand of the single form of tenancy must be lifted, and the more socially desirable, and socially desired, aim of home-ownership put in its place. If a national referendum were to be held on the simple question 'Do you wish to own your own home?' there is no doubt as to the answer that would be given. It must be made possible for that most legitimate of aims — as basic as the right to work — to be fulfilled.

The very desirability of home-ownership to most people in this country can be proved by the simple statistics that illustrate the growth of owner-occupation over even the last thirty years. We now live in a country where more than half the total number of households are bought with a freehold, or long leasehold owned by the family; until recent developments in the housing market we have been in the situation where that percentage has systematically increased. The reasons why people buy or long-lease houses are very simple. They resent the constant financial drain and strain of rents, whether it be to a landlord in the private sector or to a council, neither of which in return give a stake in a major capital investment or the psycho/sociological benefits which home-ownership confers, and which social housing lacks.

There is the radical view that socially owned houses should be in fact simply given away to their occupants — to enfranchise perhaps a third of our citizens at a stroke, and give them, by redistributing wealth in the form of the valuable capital asset represented by a house, a sudden substantial stake in the country. Other, less adventurous, schemes to the same end will undoubtedly prove more immediately practical. The Conservative Party's armoury must be filled with weapons additional to the sale of council houses alone, heavy gun of the home-ownership movement though that may be.

The argument over the sale of council houses advanced by the Labour Party has, of course, been dogmatic rather than financial. For it is widely realised that the sale of council houses, to those who don't need to rent and can buy, frees valuable resources which can then be used to build more council houses for those who do need them; and also to speed up clearance, rehousing and programmes for the rehabilitation of outdated stock. In round figures, the subsidy to owner-occupiers via tax relief is about £300 p.a., while the subsidy on a new-built council house is at least £1000 p.a., a figure which varies regionally: now, in 1976, it is well over £1000 p.a. in inner London. It is simply cheaper for society to support home-ownership than social housing. Sale of council houses also relieves an authority of many of the debt charges on the loans financing council house construction, and frees it of maintenance and service charges. And, what is more, the average life of a council house tenancy is 20—30 years, so it is again simply wrong to say that the sale of council houses would dry up the supply of rented tenancies — rather it would free money to build houses now for people who need them now. These basic facts are being recognised now even by some Socialist Ministers, and indeed in March 1976 the Socialist-controlled London Boroughs Association gave evidence supporting some sale of council houses to a Department of the

Environment inquiry on housing finance.

Of course mortgages would have to be supplied for such purchases, by the councils themselves or by the Government. These would be expensive. But they would none the less be cheaper than endless construction of council houses on 60-year-term finance. Indeed, such mortgages would be a good way of attacking lengthening waiting lists. The assumption that it is cheaper to help people to buy their own houses than have them as council tenants is as valid in this case as it is in that of the direct sale of council houses to sitting tenants. For councils could well offer interest-free second mortgages to those who can afford a substantial part, though not all, of a mortgage. It would be cheaper for them in effect to 'top up' the first mortgage in this way than build, and then for ever maintain, a house for the person who was within reach of, though not quite at, the point at which he or she could become a home-owner. It need not stop there. Were it possible to devise ways of sharing the debt burden incurred by public authorities when building new council houses, it would be possible also to offer some of the benefits of home-ownership to those who cannot ever, or for a while, earn enough to purchase outright. The attraction of council house tenants taking a part in the equity of their house would be that they, too, could benefit in an inflationary situation by having their commitment to pay for housing based upon the historic cost of their house, and not upon the average cost of houses built by the public authority, a figure which naturally rises as building costs and land costs rise over the lifetime of a tenant's occupancy. Part-equity schemes, such as those pioneered in Birmingham, spread the financial burdens and the financial benefits of housing, and increase freedom of choice. Such schemes are also flexible. They allow for conversion to, on the one hand, full ownership of equity for those whose circumstances change for the better, and reversion to full tenancy for those whose circumstances unfortunately decline.

At this point I should like to quote part of a letter published in one typical local paper: '. . . current house prices now put house purchase beyond the reach of most young couples, *except perhaps for the privileged few with inherited wealth.*' [D. Norman, *Oxford Times*, 12 September 1975: italics mine.] A view such as this is sadly prevalent. It is also wrong. It is cheaper to help people buy houses than to provide houses for renting. But there seems to be a threshold of understanding on this matter that not many even in local authorities, let alone the general public, have breached. It is of vital importance to the whole distorted world of social housing finance that this breach be made as soon as possible, and the sacred cow of universal social housing driven out, to be replaced by a more varied and variable philosophy of tenure and ownership that would meet social and financial needs more exactly.

Straight home-ownership, important strides forward though it has made in the last fifty years, has not solved our housing problem. Selling or part selling council houses alone has not and will not do so either. Yet, by giving tax relief on mortgages, governments of both the left and the right have been as interventionist as they have in council housing. We certainly need to have faith in the building societies even when times are bad, because they seem to remain the best means of aggregating the savings of the small investor and channelling them into the housing market. But home-ownership has still not solved the housing problems of the lower-paid despite the introduction of the option mortgage scheme. Even if they have approximately the income to pay off a mortgage they often have trouble with the deposit. We must never forget that the home-owner who bought before 1970 has not only made a mighty and untaxed capital gain, but is also making repayments in greatly depreciated pounds. On the other hand, the vagaries of the free market have subsequently dictated that those who bought after that date may no longer really be able to afford to pay instalments on an asset whose capital value may actually be declining. Any unfavourable change in tax would fall with devastating force on the new mortgagor. The future course of inflation and demand make it impossible to predict the effect of tax changes upon a twenty-year or twenty-five-year mortgage bargain. To ask mortgagors to suddenly pay a very markedly different set of repayments, perhaps even by withdrawing tax relief, is as unreasonable and socially unjust as asking council house tenants ever to pay the real cost-rent for their properties. And it is mistaken to accept that tax relief on mortgages and subsidy payments to council house tenants are directly comparable expenditures. Tax relief is different really from a direct subsidy in that a subsidy payment to someone represents someone else's tax bill, whilst tax relief merely means that an individual is allowed to keep more of his own income — rather than take someone else's — if he or she chooses to spend his or her money in a certain way. Help with a deposit seems to be of paramount importance for the marginal potential home-owner, and a cash grant of several hundred pounds, matching savings pound for pound or based on some other formula, would be an important start. But it must be controlled, recognising the effects on a sensitive housing market that a sudden demand for cheaper houses could have in an inflationary age, though private construction could undoubtedly take up the sudden demand if planning procedures were speeded up and smaller units at higher densities allowed more freely.

Lastly, much of the future of home-ownership seems to depend on factors outside our direct control. The world economic situation and the vagaries of the money market directly affect the cash positions of building societies one way or another. Stabilisation funds between one (good) and the next (possibly bad) year seem a good idea, and better than short-term panic government intervention, via loans to keep mortgage rates down, such as both administrations have been party to of late. The whole issue needs the most sensitive handling so that the market is not distorted. For instance, one attractive solution might lie in amending the composite rate of tax on deposits with building societies in order to raise more funds; but even in the short term this could have damaging effects. For not only the housing market, but parts of the money market could be distorted: building societies would suddenly become very attractive investment opportunities with the resultant inflow of funds. Building societies then, flush with funds, would be in a 1971/72 situation with a glut of lending releasing pent-up demand and driving up house prices, thus taking the possibility of home-ownership away from those at the bottom end of the market who need it most.

In conclusion what is clearly needed and wanted by all are policies to enable people to buy who have never been able to before. It is what they want, what they need, what is cheapest for society to help them with, and what produces the most socially desirable results and the greatest individual happiness. We also need to encourage builders to build more homes more quickly, to stabilise the mortgage market, and to make home improvement easier; we need to make the best use of our existing housing stock; and to aim throughout our whole housing sphere for quality in an agreeable environment.

For there is no good to be gained in having good housing in a poor environment without open space, play areas, etc.; even less in having poorly designed, but quickly constructed, housing. Certainly, as Graham Richards points out in Chapter 10, the Conservative Party as such does not have the reputation of being a good conservationist. We do not have the reputation for removing traffic from city centres, putting freight on to the railways, or preventing urban sprawl. Our — the Party's — ecological philosophy needs deeper thought. It has been left to others to point the way to an environmental awareness. And, as Richards says, 'during the years of power, 1970 to 1974, the Conservatives acquired the image not just of being the friends of big business, but of being the friends of the developer who cared least for any conservation policy.'

It goes without saying then that any great crusade to build more homes to house the homeless at all, to house the poorly housed better, and to spread home-ownership, must be within the effective environmental policy. The environment is not amenable to conservation by blanket diktat. It is without doubt the arena for one-off decisions about one-off situations — to demolish or not; to change elevation or not; to close this street, or ban cars from that, or not; to build this inner relief road or not; to allow that development at that density or not. Speeding-up of planning procedures has been advocated in this chapter, but those who advocate it must realise that such changes must be accompanied by equal changes in the degree of environmental protection. There is material enough for a separate chapter on what these detailed provisions might be, too detailed for essays such as these. But we need to take greater care of our crowded island in which more and more houses must be built, so that the conflicts of land use, housing need and conservation can be resolved to ensure good housing in a good environment.

8 The Social Services

ANN SPOKES

*The Scheme of Society for which we stand is the establishment
and maintenance of a basic minimum standard of life and labour
below which a man or woman of good will, however old or weak,
will not be allowed to fall.*

Winston Churchill, Party Conference, 1947

This was the quotation with which the writers of the 'One Nation' group
began their book in 1950, epitomising the Tory creed in its approach to
social problems. Later Churchill explained further the difference between
what could be described as the Socialist queue and the Conservative
ladder. 'If people ask "what happens if anyone slips off the ladder?" our
reply is: "We shall have a good net and the finest social ambulance service
in the world." ' [Broadcast, October 1951]

Conservative philosophy on social services differs markedly from the
Labour Party's. The basic defect in the latter's interpretation of the
Welfare State (which for some reason they think they invented) is that
they believe in an average standard of universal, indiscriminate benefits for
all. Their philosophy assumes a bottomless pit of resources and results in
welfare being spread so thin that those in the greatest need may not get
sufficient, or go without altogether. In other words, this view produces
holes in the net to fall through.

Conservatives have always recognised that help to those in need is more
important than universal help to all. Because it is impossible to do
everything one would wish then priorities must be fixed. Priorities should
be planned in advance and not suddenly altered to suit expediency.
Sudden backtracking when the money runs out is not only wasteful, but it
can result in needless hardship. What can be spent must match what there
is in the kitty. One cannot help the weak without wealth. Runaway
inflation, bad government, the stifling of initiative and slow industrial
growth all mean less wealth. If wealth and profit are dirty words the
inevitable result is that people in need will have to go without. Tories have
always recognised the necessity for balancing the needs of the poor against
the need to encourage the rich. 'Maintaining the social services . . . can be

done only if there is a speedy increase in national production . . . whether
this increase in production can be obtained or not will . . . depend to a
large extent on all those engaged in industry. We must call on them for a
great effort to save our social services.' [*One Nation*, p. 92] A more recent
example of this theme was expressed by Norman Fowler at the Party
Conference in October 1975: 'Labour assume that economic policy is
somehow separate from provision for those in need. But that is the
greatest nonsense . . . The greatest need is resources and those will only
come when industry is able to produce the wealth.'

The Conservative approach to social services has always been essentially
practical, pragmatic and — perhaps surprisingly, considering the inspiration
was Disraeli's — usually unromantic. Disraeli devised what Iain Macleod
was later to describe as 'the blueprint of Tory Democracy' by substituting
an 's' for a 'v' in a Latin quotation — 'sanitas sanitatum, omnia sanitas'
(Manchester, 3 April 1872). Lord Randolph Churchill, writing in the
Fortnightly Review of May 1883, said of Disraeli's initiative:

> By it is shadowed forth, and in it is embraced, a social revolution
> which, passing by and diverting attention from the wild longings for
> organic change . . . comprises Lord Salisbury's plans for the ameliora-
> tion of the poor, carries with it Lord Carnarvon's idea of compulsory
> National Insurance . . . constructs people's parks, collects and opens to
> the masses museums, libraries, art galleries, does not disdain the public
> wash-houses of Mr. Jesse Collings.

It was even then recognised that none of these things could be done
without wealth and Lord Randolph therefore went on to explain: 'Public
and private thrift must animate the whole, for it is from public thrift alone
that their results can be utilized and appreciated.' In the years which
followed (1874—80) the Conservatives put in hand their first great
programme of social reform and so unromantic did it appear to some that
is was described by one Liberal MP as a 'policy of sewage'.

The principle that it was the duty of the Government to look after the
health of the people was in fact first recognised by a Conservative
Government as early as 1845 when the Board of Supervision — the
forerunner of the Ministry of Health — was set up. But it was not until
1875 that Disraeli's Government passed the first Public Health Act, which
was the real foundation of public health administration. This was soon
followed by the Sale of Food and Drugs Act and further measures were
passed by Conservative Governments between 1876 and 1904 to improve
the health and welfare of the British people. There was a host of measures
dealing with such varied problems as clean meat, rivers, swimming baths
and the prevention of infectious diseases. After the First World War there
were various provisions for the blind, and the tuberculous, and for smoke
abatement, together with the registration of nursing and maternity homes

and the maternity and child welfare services. They all followed Disraeli's dictum that the 'first consideration of a Minister should be the health of the people'. Even Lloyd George admitted that the introduction of non-contributory old age pensions in 1908 owed much to the pioneer work done by Joseph Chamberlain, and it was the other Chamberlain — Neville — who is associated with the great Conservative legislation of 1925 which brought in contributory pensions.

The years between the two wars were ones of tremendous expansion for the social services. The only time when there was any serious check on progress was in the immediate period of crisis after the 1929—31 period of Socialist Government. By April 1939 a leading Scottish Socialist (Sir Patrick Dollan) was able to say: 'I know of no country where the Social Services are so high, so varied and so well supported as they are in this country'. Progress was possible so long as the economic condition of Britain remained sound. One may well ask why the myth of 'Tory misrule' between the wars gathered such momentum that by the 1945 General Election even some Conservatives were ready to doubt that there had been such advances in social reform. This belief was still widespread in 1950 as the writers of *One Nation* pointed out: 'Today, people are fond of saying that Britain leads the world in the field of social services. We tend to forget that this was so even before the War'. Socialist propaganda started in the early years of the 1939—45 war. Thanks to short memories and the fact that the younger electors would have been too young to experience them, the myth of the bad Tory years was spread. It was so successful that people were surprised when the truth about our progress in the social services during the period was published. The ground was well prepared by careful repetition of the legend throughout the war years when there was supposed to be a political truce.

At about the same time (1941) as Socialists were already initiating their propaganda about the years of 'Tory misrule' Sir William (later Lord) Beveridge was appointed by the Government to plan for the integration of the different social service schemes which then existed into a coherent whole. Speaking about the Beveridge Report and the then Government's 'Four Years' Plan' in 1943 Churchill said: 'You must rank me and my colleagues as strong partisans of national compulsory insurance for all classes from the cradle to the grave'. Though all was prepared for the legislation to go ahead there was only time for the Family Allowances Act before the General Election of 1945 brought in a Socialist Government. As the Bills were passed, there was only controversy on one part of the proposals — the National Health Service — and even here the argument was not about the principle, but only about the way Aneurin Bevan conceived it. Thus the social legislation in the immediate post-war years — planned by the mainly Conservative coalition Government — followed the tradition of the inter-war period. Beveridge himself paid tribute to this in his report when he described our system of health and unemployment benefits and pensions as 'not surpassed and hardly rivalled in any other country in the world'. Yet the myth that the inter-war period had been a time of continuous grinding poverty and appallingly bad and worsening social conditions was so widespread that Socialists were able to spread the fear that any future Tory Government would inevitably cut the social services. In 1949 the *ABC of the Crisis*, an official Labour Party publication, said that if the Tories were in power they would 'slash the social services benefiting the poor and drive the workers to the point of starvation'. In fact, Conservative legislation in the social services was never spasmodic, but has been continuous from the nineteenth century, through the 1930s and 1940s, to the present day. It has all been designed to improve the condition of the people without stifling initiative and enterprise.

Tories have always emphasised that the social services cannot be improved without the necessary resources. 'Sentiment should not be allowed to obscure realities' [*One Nation*, p. 64]. On the other hand, it has been observed: 'Socialists think that politics consists of meditating in the abstract about what is good for Man, then having a quick glance at the world as it is in order to find out how much of this you can persuade particular men to put up with.' [T. E. Utley, *The Conservatives and the Critics*, 1956]. The 'One Nation' Group summed up the difference between the approach of the two main parties:

> There is a fundamental disagreement between Conservatives and Socialists on the question of social policy. Socialists would give the same benefits to everyone whether or not the help is needed, and indeed whether or not the Country's resources are adequate. We believe that we must first help those in need. Socialists believe that it should provide an average standard. We believe that it should provide a minimum standard above which people should be free to rise as their industry, their thrift, their ability and their genius may take them.

Socialists can never accept this view because their beliefs are based on the theory that if everyone cannot have it then no one should have it. This is seen in other fields; for example, if all cannot go to direct grant schools then no one should; if everyone cannot own a bit of land then no one should; if everyone cannot afford to buy their own council house than no one should; if everyone cannot have a quiet, smoke-free hospital room then no one should; and even, recently, in some quarters — if everyone cannot own a car then all should go by bus or train. Just as taxation can level down, so they always hope that the welfare state can do the same. Conservatives, on the other hand, as R. A. Butler said in the introduction to *The New Conservatism* (1955), would rather ask: 'how can we ensure that the Welfare State works to elevate the many rather than level the few?'

Resources will always be scarce because in the field of health and social

services there is always an increasing number of things we would like to
do. If we insist on providing a flat level of benefits for everybody it may
mean doing less than we should for those with special needs and special
problems. A flexible approach is therefore essential. Edward Heath saw
this need for more flexibility in the use of resources in the social services
so that they could be better directed to the real needs [Birmingham,
February 1966]. He saw the need to get the economy right not as an end
in itself, but as a way of ridding the country of the remaining pockets of
need and poverty. This theme had run through Conservative policies in the
1950s. The 1950 election manifesto had proclaimed that 'the social
services, born of Parliaments with Conservative and Liberal majorities, rest
upon the productive effort of British industry and agriculture. The
Socialists have by inflation reduced their value and compromised their
future.' The 1951 manifesto had recognised that the surest way to preserve
our social services was to increase our national output ('Britain Strong and
Free'). And in 1952, after their first year back in office, Conservatives
wrote (in 'We Shall Win Through'): 'Social services, paid for out of the
national wealth, can be maintained and expanded only if that wealth is
maintained and expanded.' The 1959 manifesto had seen the possibility of
doubling the standard of living in a generation not just as a material aim in
itself, but an achievement which would form the basis not only of rising
living standards, but of social reform and the creation of one nation.

In the Introduction to 'For All the People' in 1972, Mr Heath said:

> Prosperity by itself is not enough. It has to be linked with fairness if it
> is to help create a better life for all . . . A social policy for *all* the people
> means making sure that extra help goes to those who need it most even
> if others who are more fortunate have to pay a little more for some of
> the services the system provides. Experience shows that they are willing
> to do so if they see the priorities are right.

This was the period of Conservative Government, with Sir Keith Joseph as
Social Services Minister, when, for the first time by any Government, help
was given to those in special need who had been omitted from the existing
insurance scheme. These included pensions for the over-80s (so long
resisted by the Socialists) and special supplements for the very old already
in the system. There was also the new invalidity benefit for the long-term
workless because of illness. Most important of all was the family income
supplement for the low wage earners — a magnificent means of solving the
problem of poverty among people too poor to pay tax who yet preferred
to work rather than draw supplementary benefit. Lord Balniel [*Must the
Children Suffer?*, 1968] described it as a system 'which concentrates help
where it is most needed; a system which is automatic and which avoids the
use of the conventional means test. Yet it is a system which identifies need

and which retains the incentive for each family to work its way up to
better standards by its own efforts.'

Constant through the years is the Conservative belief that help should
be concentrated first and foremost on those whose needs are greatest. The
most easily recognisable people in need are those who have long-term
requirements — large families on low incomes, widows, the homeless, the
chronically sick, permanently handicapped people and large numbers of
the elderly population. But we must remember that there may also be
needs of a temporary, but nevertheless severe, nature occurring among
people who are normally independent, because of sudden illness, bereave-
ment, accidents, redundancy and so on. One may be the healthiest of
individuals and then find that because of unforeseen illness, earnings
suddenly cease. A mother with three young children may suddenly find
herself thrown on the mercy of the State because her young husband has
been killed in a motor accident. He may have been earning a good wage,
but there are no savings, the house may still be mortgaged and household
equipment still be on hire purchase. However affluent the society there
will always be help needed for such people. Many people insure privately
against such eventualities, but there are many who cannot afford to do so
even if they wanted to. Churchill recognised that thrift is not always
possible when one lives near the breadline. This is why there must always
be the basic social services on top of which individuals may provide their
own. This is the answer to those who say: 'Shouldn't we only help those
who cannot help themselves?' It is not nearly so easy to ascertain who
they are or who they might be. In any case, need is not always for money,
but for support, expert advice, shelter and so on.

One of the great dilemmas is how to assess need. The one means test
which people accept as necessary is income tax. The product of income
tax should be what there is to spend, not what the Exchequer thinks the
Community will bear — paper money if the money is not there. As Sir
Brandon Rhys Williams said in 1967 [*The New Social Contract*] :

> The income tax should be the only investigation of means. It is a form
> of means test that everybody should be willing to submit to without
> any sense of loss of freedom, privacy or self-respect. The State should
> not seek any other way of probing the circumstances of individuals or
> curbing the increase in private property or wealth. To impose a means
> test on both sides of the ledger — i.e. on the share of a man's income
> which the state takes in tax as well as on the benefits that it pays in
> exchange, is simply a form of double taxation. Its effect is to penalise
> success.

He went on to say that benefits should not be limited to those who are
unable to pay for them any more than insurance companies should only
meet in full the claims of destitute insurers.

One often hears about abuses of the system, and abuses there are bound to be. But there has always been a far worse problem – the ignorance of those in need about the services to which they are entitled. For the one person who abuses the system there are today probably a thousand who need help, but do not get it. This is why a simplification of the system by some form of tax credit scheme which would virtually solve the problem of take-up is probably the wisest course.

Mention has been made in the introduction to this chapter of the Conservative insistence on growth as a necessary corollary of benefits – wealth to pay for welfare. Lord Randolph Churchill first touched upon this in 1883 and it has never been far from the minds of Conservatives in the context of their policy for the social services. We have always quarrelled with the Socialist view that the welfare state is a 'kind of bran-tub out of which more and more benefits can be pulled if only one votes for the right party' [Rhys Williams, op.cit., p. 17]. The seemingly endless and insatiable demands of the health and social services meant that Tories in office were continually having to explain that much as they would like to increase the money spent still further it could not be done. R. A. Butler, attacked for his 'savage cuts' at a time when Exchequer expenditure on the social services was increasing rapidly, explained [*Tradition and Change*, 1954] : 'unless we allow men and women to rise as far as they may, and so allow our society to be served by . . . the richness of developed differences, we shall not have the means to earn our national living, let alone to afford a Welfare State.' Despite the high priority given to the social services (and in the early 1970s the Conservatives gave them a higher priority than any Government in history), the demands were continually increasing. It was pointed out that in order for yet more resources to be found there would have to be higher growth rates – one cannot help the weak without wealth.

'There is no other way of developing the industrial base on which the Government's whole programme of social services depend than by increasing the national wealth. In the long run social services depend on an economic foundation and growth'. True Tory philosophy – yes; but not said by a Conservative. These words were spoken by Harold Wilson when addressing the annual meeting of the National Council of Social Service in December 1975. His Social Services Secretary, Barbara Castle, said much the same the month before to the local authorities' Social Services Conference. It remains to be seen whether such words – new to the Socialist lips – will ever appear in a Labour Party policy document. Sir Keith Joseph said something very similar to a meeting of social workers when he was in the position later held by Mrs Castle, and came under scathing attack. Today the words of wisdom of Conservatives which have been repeated decade after decade are now at last understood and repeated by Socialists without even a twist of the neck. It is, of course, too much to hope that they will take one step further down the road and accept that in order to achieve growth one needs to encourage thrift, enterprise and individual intiative. As T. E. Utley put it in *The Conservatives and the Critics* in 1956:

> ... there are certain elementary truths which politicians who are not economists are apt to neglect. One of them is that the minority upon whom all vast increases in production depend are peculiarly susceptible to the influence of profit ... [Another is] the need to stimulate exceptional talent by exceptional reward ... The desire for individual profit and the fear of individual loss are extremely powerful motives.

In recent decades there has always been an increase in the annual amount allotted in real terms to the health and social services. Today — in a time of financial crisis — there is to be little or no growth at all. To make sure that what money is allocated is used to the best advantage forward planning of priorities is essential. But this will also need to be flexible, with a number of options to be considered at any given moment of time. Priorities must be clearly recognised. 'Socialists pay lip service to the need for priorities; in practice they have lacked the courage to enforce them and the administrative ability to make services work'. [*One Nation*, p. 10] To spend on one part of the service will mean cutting out another and in the Health Service this may mean depriving ill people of care they need. As Dr Trevor Weston wrote [*How is the Health Service?*, 1972]: 'The public would like and are tacitly allowed to believe that rationing in medical care does not occur under the National Health Service. In fact, it occurs all the time and to an extent that would come as an unpleasant surprise to most people'.

It is in the field of the personal social services that the inability to recognise the need for flexibility and for continual reassessment of priorities is already having unfortunate effects. The personal social services are today in a serious difficulty because demands continue to grow without the necessary resources. There has been a spate of Government legislation in this field which the local authority social service departments have been expected to implement without sufficient financial backing. For example, the Chronically Sick and Disabled Act (which was a Private Member's Bill) had provisions which, although beyond criticism in themselves, were never matched by sufficient resources to carry them out. Also, certain unhappy cases, such as those of Maria Colwell and Steven Meurs, have hit the headlines so that many social workers feel vulnerable and threatened by a society which is only too ready to blame those who make the mistakes when the critics have the advantage of being wise after the event.

If social service departments are expected to be responsible for all the needs of society they are put in an impossible position. It is in such a situation that priorities are not sufficiently considered. In these circumstances it would not be surprising if in an effort to prevent further cases of child battering some elderly people were to suffer by a shift of skilled casework from old to young. It is wrong that priorities should be determined by the fear of the very occasional tragedy, however easy it is for angry critics to say that all such tragedies should be prevented.

The personal social services, brought together in single local authority departments, still suffer from the fact that everything is expected of them with little priority planning. Elected members on local authority committees are understandably saying that it is the job of the professionals to choose the priorities in social work and it is equally understandable that the latter say it is the job of the politicians to do so. In a situation where there is no growth in financial resources, but a continual increase in demand, it is not surprising that both are reluctant to shoulder the ultimate responsibility for making the choices in other than straightforward capital schemes. In a service which should have an inbuilt flexibility it is sad that pressures are preventing it from reacting to the inevitable new problems and that duties laid upon it by Parliament often put it in a strait-jacket. Qualified staff are a scarce resource and yet in most places they are under such pressure that there is little time spent on taking a step back to ask the essential question: 'Are they being used in the right way on the right tasks?' Job analysis is virtually non-existent. The service is not only manpower-intensive, but it is very untrained compared with other professions. About 40 per cent of field social workers are trained, but the figure is below 17 per cent for residential staff. It will be short-sighted if at a time of no growth in financial resources training is not given the priority it deserves.

One cannot conclude a chapter on the social services without a mention of voluntary organisations in this field. Conservatives have, throughout their history, recognised the important place which voluntary services play in any scheme for the elevation of the condition of the people and it would be difficult to find a Conservative policy document on the social services which does not mention them. We have always realised that the State cannot and never should provide all our needs. Just as, in the words of Iain Macleod [Nigel Fisher's biography, p. 271], it is necessary for 'private shoulders to bear a large share of the burden of social insurance', so we rely on the 'private hands' of voluntary organisations as partners in the social services. Recently, there has been an encouraging increase in the number of 'self-help' groups alongside the older-established bodies.

Most of the early social services were first introduced by groups of volunteers, and much pioneering work still goes on today. An American writer once described our system as 'pragmatic, optimistic imperfectionism' because we have tended to leap before looking, but the result is that we have begun services which the Americans are now glad to copy.

Volunteers already play such an important part in community care that without them the strain on the health and social services would be unbearable. However, it is still not sufficiently recognised that volunteers often need to be informed about how to offer their help; they need to be properly briefed and expertly placed and kept interested and enthusiastic. The voluntary organisations (as distinct from the individual volunteers) must be equal to this task. They need at least some full-time professional paid staff and this means grant-aid. Still too prevalent — in some parts of the country it is worse than others — is the view that voluntary organisations should not be run by trained staff unless they can be obtained on the cheap or for nothing. This is a short-sighted policy because voluntary help is a precious commodity and the recruitment, training and placing of volunteers is a difficult and demanding task. Properly directed grant-aid will save resources in the end.

Much more will need to be done in future to enable the staff of voluntary agencies to be trained for their work. Because many voluntary organisations are small it will not be easy for relief staff and sufficient financial resources to be found. Conservatives, believing that voluntary organisations have a part to play, will have to turn their attention to the need for Government support in this field.

The social services are changing all the time and the needs are changing. Any alteration in the direction of provision in one service, whether it be in health, personal social services, housing, insurance or income maintenance, inevitably affects the others. Our policies must, therefore, be flexible and adaptable. The main thing is that our principles remain firm. The key Conservative principle is balancing the needs of the weak against the need to encourage the strong. If one loses the help of the strong, then it is harder to help the weak. The difference between ourselves and the Socialists is that they never seem to worry about stifling the responsibilities of those who can fend for themselves if only given the chance. They have never thought it mattered if there was little freedom and less opportunity for people to provide for themselves and their families. With only so much to spend we must decide which needs have priority, even if today's priority may cease to be one tomorrow. We should endeavour to maintain a true balance between a self-help state and a helping state.

9 Education

VERNON BOGDANOR

The kind of educational policy one supports depends upon the kind of society one wants to live in. The great educational thinkers of the past — Locke and Rousseau, Newman and J. S. Mill — placed their thought within the context of how men ought to live in society. Conservatives believe in a free and diversified society in which there is a subtle interplay between individual freedom and social responsibility. Whereas the spirit of educational reformers tends to the intolerant, Conservatives find it difficult to believe that any single panacea, whether egalitarian or *laissez-faire*, can resolve the complex problems of a living education system. Education policy must inevitably resolve itself into balancing and weighing up the value of different and mutually incompatible principles of action.

In a free society a vital aim of education policy must be to create an enlightened citizenry. A democratic government, therefore, has the responsibility of providing this framework for citizenship. It must ensure that all are equipped with the basic elements of literacy and numeracy. It must seek to develop in all its citizens the critical standards through which they can distinguish the true from the false, the lasting from the meretricious. The pursuit of quality, then, should be a central objective of Conservative policy.

Even as recently as fifteen years ago, the pursuit of such an objective would have appeared unexceptionable, and would have been accepted as a truism by all those involved in education. For the 1944 Education Act and later reforms in the examination system had succeeded in producing a consensus amongst politicians, educationalists, teachers and parents. This consensus embraced both the structure and the content as well as the method of education; it embraced what was to be taught and in what kind of school it was to be taught, how it was to be taught and how examined.

This consensus collapsed during the 1960s with the rapid advance of the comprehensive system, and an associated scepticism concerning the value of traditional teaching methods and examinations. These changes led to a great divide in education policy. On one side of the divide stood the new educational establishment — administrators, both local and national, leaders of the teachers' unions (though not, be it noted, most of their members), educational journalists and progressive politicians. On the other side of the divide stood parents, doubtful and confused. The result, on both sides, has been incomprehension and bafflement.

The new educational establishment tried to develop a new consensus, based upon the enlightened wisdom of the 1960s. The role of the Conservative Party during this period was a passive one; it found itself unable to combat the new consensus; some Conservatives, dazzled by contemporary fashions, were happy to accept it: but most Conservatives remained obstinately attached to the *status quo*. The sad result was that the Conservative Party became defensive and apologetic about education; its policies became concessionary and not creative.

But the attempt to build a new consensus failed, not through the opposition of the Conservative Party, but because the two central assumptions of the new consensus came to be disproved by experience. The first assumption was that institutional and organisational changes would lead, not only to higher standards in education, but also to desirable changes in society. For the intention behind the expansion of the 1960s was not only to increase opportunity, but also to create a more egalitarian society. Educational reform was held to constitute the best mechanism for curing a host of social evils; it would relieve poverty, break the hold of the established class system, and solve the problem of cultural deprivation. Behind many of the proposals for reform lay a crude environmentalist picture of human nature and of the causes of failure.

This conception of education was strongly supported by the so-called 'moderate' wing of the Labour Party, by men such as Mr Prentice and Mr Crosland. Aware that nationalisation was hardly likely to prove a popular rallying-cry amongst an increasingly sophisticated electorate, Mr Crosland in his book *The Future of Socialism* published in 1956, sought to replace nationalisation by educational reform as the central theme of modern socialism. 'Socialism', he argued, 'is about equality'; and equality was to be achieved, not through nationalisation, but through reforms such as the abolition of the public schools and the introduction of a comprehensive system of education.

The slogan of equality in education would prove far more popular than nationalisation since it would appeal to motives of envy and hostility to learning which, as Matthew Arnold well knew, always lay beneath the surface of democratic politics. It was indeed Arnold, who, after visiting Switzerland, reported that it was a society that was 'socialistic, in the sense in which that word expresses a principle hostile to the interests of true society — *the elimination of superiorities*'.

Unfortunately, however, recent experience in Britain and the United States shows clearly that neither expansion nor egalitarianism have succeeded in eradicating social problems. The work of the American sociologist, Christopher Jencks, in his book *Inequality*, has shown fairly conclusively that variations in the education system have little effect upon the educational opportunity open to an individual; and, therefore, reform of the system is not an appropriate method of dealing with social problems. 'We cannot', according to Jencks, 'blame economic inequality on differences between schools, since differences between schools seem to have very little effect on any measurable attribute on those who attend them.' The Coleman Report, *Equality of Educational Opportunity* (1966), showed that few of the individual differences in educational achievement were accounted for by anything that went on in the schools. Therefore further moves towards egalitarianism in education were unlikely to do much good, either to educational standards or to society itself. It is for this reason that expensive programmes such as Head Start have so totally failed to make any impact upon educational deprivation.

They can, however, do harm. In Britain, the establishment view has failed to lead to an improvement in the quality of education, but it may bear some responsibility for the decline in standards, widely suspected by many parents and observers of the educational scene. For the trouble is that the orthodoxy of the 1960s exaggerated the influence of the school as an agency of social reform. It placed upon schools and teachers widespread responsibilities for curing social ills, which they were ill-equipped to bear. Having been asked to perform a diverse and ill-defined range of tasks, it is not surprising that the schools have been unable to succeed in their central task of providing basic literacy and numeracy for all children. Like governments, schools have been over-burdened with impossible tasks; and in both cases, the attempt to achieve the impossible has militated against fulfilling the purposes for which the institutions exist.

The second plank of educational orthodoxy was that educational advance should be measured by the quantity of resources and the amount of money spent on education. Concern for the quantity of provision came to replace concern for the quality of education; and the conflict between the parties was less over aims and priorities than over how much was being spent on the education service. The Labour and Conservative parties became involved in an auction, each outbidding the other in its generosity. Educational problems were to be solved by throwing money at them and hoping that they would go away.

In *Inflation and Priorities*, edited by Rudolf Klein for the Centre for Studies in Social Policy, it is stated that: 'Since the beginning of the 1950s education has been one of Britain's growth industries. Between 1953 and 1973 the Gross Domestic Product increased by 74.7%, but expenditure on education went up by 274.5%.' Few, however, would be prepared to claim that the quality of education improved by anything like the same proportion. For, of course, the amount spent on education has never been a good guide to the quality of provision. As Mrs Thatcher remarked at the 1973 Conservative Conference, 'statistics do not reveal everything about education, and you do not in fact necessarily achieve greater quality by just pouring in more money. It costs just as much to train a bad teacher as it does to train a good teacher.'

It is now clear that the period of rapid growth in educational expenditure is over, but so also, if Jencks and Coleman are to be believed, is the assumption that more and more schooling for more and more children will solve either our educational or our social problems. The indefinite extension of education for all would be unlikely to have any beneficial effects. The raising of the school leaving age was probably the last step upon that particular road. We travel along it only because we do not know where else to go.

It need not, therefore, be a cause for dismay that education is no longer to be a growth industry. For both egalitarianism and expansionism have been shown to be false gods. With the collapse of the establishment consensus, the debate moves, as it should, to the issue of priorities, an issue veiled by the competition over statistics. Behind the consensus lay a method of thinking which has proved harmful to any serious appraisal of educational aims — I refer to the *mechanistic* or *economic* approach of the administrators, which needs to be replaced by a very different approach; so that we look again at individual children, at how well they are learning and how well they are being given a motivation for further study. We must, then, look again at what it is we want our education system to achieve.

How are priorities to be decided and how is the aim of quality in education to be achieved? The beginning of wisdom, for most Conservatives, is that central government possesses no special ability to determine priorities for different localities with different needs. As Rudolf Klein has noticed (*Inflation and Priorities*), 'the new economic situation calls into question the whole relationship between central and local government'. Are priorities to be decided centrally or locally? Centralisers will argue in favour of firm government control of priorities; only within a system in which responsibility clearly flows from the centre, they will say, will it be possible to ensure value for money and financial accountability. A corollary of this view is a contemptuous rejection of the capacities of local authorities to manage their affairs efficiently, and a suspicion of any form of devolution of power that weakens central control.

This position has, however, come to look increasingly threadbare as the weaknesses of central government have, in recent years, been made apparent — the Crossman diaries have played a salutary role in this process. For it is precisely in the areas of strategic control and financial accountability that central government has failed most lamentably. It has failed to plan successfully for the number of students in higher education and it has failed to estimate correctly the demand for teachers. These failures have occurred because central government has become overloaded; the machine has become clogged up with the huge variety of problems it is expected to solve. It is, therefore, a mistake to believe that central government possesses some special knowledge or expertise enabling it to decide priorities for the whole country. As Thomas Jefferson once argued, if we were directed from Washington where to sow and reap we would soon want bread. At the same time, people have felt themselves become more and more alienated from government. In a modern bureaucratic society individuals feel under constant pressure to reassert their identity. This has led not only to the rise of nationalism in Scotland and Wales, but also to a revival of local feeling. The increasing importance and strength of local and environmental pressure groups over the last decade bears striking witness to this feeling.

This has two implications. The first is that priorities should be decided as far as possible at local level; there should be the maximum possible decentralisation of decision-making. A Conservative should not try to offer a set of priorities in the form of a national blueprint, the same for Birmingham as for Bournemouth, for Aberdeen as for Aberystwyth. If different areas have different needs, then the appropriate policy-mix for each area is best decided at the level of the locality and not at the centre.

Secondly, the decentralisation of decision-making in education would be of benefit to central government itself. Conservatives have always believed in a strong State; but the State at present is weak, because over-extended, because it has been given tasks which it is not equipped to undertake. A genuine devolution of power, promised at the time of local government reform, would help to secure a strong State, strong because trimmed of excess and pared down for efficient action.

At the same time, the diffusion of power makes people more willing to trust central authority in those areas where it retains competence. Where all power is centralised, popular resentment will concentrate on weakening the State, but where the State restricts itself to its central tasks it has some chance of retaining respect. The contrasting attitudes to the State in over-centralised France and decentralised Britain show very clearly how centralisation is likely to weaken legitimacy rather than to strengthen it.

In the interests, then, both of education and of government itself, Conservatives should seek ways of strengthening the autonomy of local authorities. The economic crisis and need for cuts in education should be used, not to remove power to the centre, but to shift it away. Education policy should be allowed to evolve in accordance with local wishes, and not be subject to excessive imposition from the centre. The defence of local autonomy in education must, therefore, remain a cornerstone of Conservative philosophy.

It would be wrong, however, to deny that local autonomy, of itself, would be unlikely to lead to an improvement in the quality of education. For local authorities have been as much under the sway of the conventional wisdom as central government. Indeed, local authorities are part of the very administrative consensus whose theoretical underpinnings have collapsed; and through their bureaucratic insensitivity to the wishes of parents, and their seeming indifference to educational standards, they bear a considerable responsibility for the widespread popular alienation from local government, an alienation which could, in the end, threaten the very basis of local autonomy itself.

Conservatives have come to realise that the unrestricted power of government can, in the modern state, only remain tolerable if it is made strictly accountable to the electorate. This is particularly difficult to achieve in the provision of public services, since there is generally no clear test of their relative efficiency through competition with the private sector. Some means must be found, therefore, to impart some real choice between alternatives, and appraisal of performance in the public sector. If the schools are to be made genuinely accountable, two things are necessary: first, a proper monitoring of standards; and secondly, measures to improve the effective influence of parents, the consumers of the education service. This must, of course, include an expansion of parental choice, since it is only where there is choice between schools that there can be some measure of the effectiveness of different schools.

The Bullock Report on reading standards highlighted the central weakness of much of the present education debate. We are arguing about standards in a vacuum, because we do not know the facts. We need to institute new methods of monitoring the progress of schools and other educational institutions. The rapid changes of the past fifteen years badly need objective evaluation. Although government has no direct responsibility for what is taught in the schools, it does have the responsibility of maintaining a continuous watch on the whole education system, and discovering how well or badly each element in the system is performing.

Formerly, the 11-plus examination, whatever its other defects, did at least act as a monitor on performance in the primary schools: the products of any primary school which failed to inculcate adequate standards of literacy and numeracy would continually perform badly at the 11-plus and the school would soon fall under public scrutiny. The abolition of the 11-plus and the weakening of the powers of the national inspectorate have, however, meant that there is no effective check on primary school standards. It is very likely that the abolition of the 11-plus has been accompanied by a decline in standards at primary school level.

What is needed then is the public monitoring of standards. This in turn requires some definition of what standards of literacy and numeracy we are trying to achieve in the primary schools; what should be the degree of literacy and numeracy of a child of 7; of 9; and of 11? Minimum national standards should be laid down which all children, except the handicapped and educationally sub-normal, should be expected to attain, at different ages. By the age of 11, children should be expected to have achieved a publicly set standard in elementary geography, history, literature and scientific knowledge. By 14, they should have mastered the rudiments of a foreign language. Of course none of this need exclude the inculcation of values such as creativity and social mixing; but these must be in addition to, and not a substitute for, the basic requirements which all have a right to expect the schools to fulfil.

In this way, accurate information could be obtained, and the debate about standards could become empirically based. This would benefit pupils, parents and teachers alike. It is true and regrettable that the professional teaching organisations have been hitherto resistant to the processes of monitoring, partly perhaps because they see in monitoring the return of a covertly disguised 11-plus. They are, however, foolish to adopt this attitude: first, because they must seek to meet the public demand to impart a stronger sense of academic standards into many primary and comprehensive schools; and secondly, because the only safeguard for teachers unfairly attacked is a full knowledge of the facts. In the end, the only honourable and satisfactory foundation for the teaching profession must be an accurate understanding of their role and public appreciation of their success in fulfilling it.

The second and complementary way in which the schools must be made accountable is through increased parental involvement. Parental involvement is best secured not through increased representation of parents on the managing bodies of schools or in parent-teacher associations — from this point of view the deliberations of the Taylor Committee are an irrelevance — but through allowing parents an increased degree of choice of school. As Dr Rhodes Boyson has so trenchantly put it, parents do not want to sit on yet another committee. They want a passport out of the school.

Conservatives have always believed that choice in education, as in other spheres of life, offers the best hope of reasoned progress. And the demand for choice is clearly becoming a feature of society which politicians ignore at their peril. An increasingly sophisticated electorate is no longer prepared to allow decisions about how its children are to be educated, be taken for it by local education officers. It is interesting to note that, when it was understood that Mrs Thatcher, as Secretary of State for Education and Science, was prepared to take parental protests seriously, there was vigorous campaigning on the part of parents to secure their rights. This demand was one which cut across conventional class barriers, embracing working-class as well as middle-class areas. 'Parent power', far from being a middle-class slogan, is one that unites the classes against the educational establishment.

Unfortunately, the law at present gives little encouragement to parental demands. Section 76 of the 1944 Education Act declares that the Secretary of State and local education authorities 'should have regard to the general principle that, so far as is compatible with the provision of efficient instruction and training and the avoidance of unreasonable public expenditure, pupils are to be educated in accordance with the wishes of their parents'; and Section 68 of the Act gives parents the right of appeal to the Secretary of State if they think a local education authority is acting 'unreasonably'.

These clauses do not, however, and were probably not intended to give parents the positive right of choice of school. Section 76 is deliberately vaguely worded so that as long as a local education authority can prove that it did 'have regard to the general principle' of parental choice, it has not been acting 'unreasonably' even if 'the general principle' has been overridden by other principles important to the local authority. The courts, rightly fearing political involvement, have consistently refused to intervene to remedy substantive, as opposed to procedural, grievances on the part of parents.

How, then, are parental rights to be guaranteed? One method that has been suggested is the voucher scheme. This scheme has a number of variants, but the basic idea is comparatively simple. Every parent of a school-age child is issued with a non-transferable voucher equal to the average cost of a child's schooling at the time. This voucher can then be 'cashed' at a school of the parent's choice. Under some schemes, 'topping-up' of the voucher is possible either through the purchase of a place at an independent school, or through a higher price being needed to purchase a place at a 'good' maintained school, the 'bad' maintained school selling places for the price of the basic voucher.

It will be seen that the premise behind the voucher scheme is that the market mechanism is the best means to secure freedom of choice for parents. It is this premise that immediately arouses suspicion: for although Conservatives believe, of course, in the vital role of the market economy, they have never worshipped the market with the dogmatic ferocity of the nineteenth-century Liberal Party or the contemporary Institute of Economic Affairs. The Cobdenite elevation of the market to the level of an ideology has little to do with true Conservatism, which distrusts all ideologies and general statements of political principle, whether those of Socialism or those of nineteenth-century liberalism. Indeed, one reason for the survival of the Conservatives as a governing party has been its healthy suspicion of ideologies, and an awareness that any truths they embody have a merely temporary validity. For finality, as Disraeli noted, is not the language of politics.

In particular, Conservatives have always recognised that it is wrong to identify freedom with the market *per se*. After all, the twentieth century has seen restrictions on the operation of markets in Britain as in other Western democracies but the result of these restrictions is that most people in these countries feel more, not less, free, and more, not less, secure.

In fact it is unrealistic to suppose that the market mechanism can be directly applied to education, since it is not possible, in the short run, to expand 'good' schools and to close down 'bad' schools. For school buildings are a commodity for which the supply is inelastic, and cannot be made, in the short run, to respond to changes in demand. Unfortunately, therefore, there must be a physical constraint in the degree of choice possible, *under any system of educational administration or finance.*

At the same time, the voucher scheme could lead to the disadvantages of schools in areas of deprivation becoming cumulative as fewer and fewer parents wish to send their children to these schools. Instead of paying extra attention to areas of deprivation, the voucher policy would shift resources to more favoured schools. Good schools would be able to raise their fees so as to exclude able children from poor backgrounds, thus accentuating the wastage of talent amongst these children. There would be a system of educational apartheid with pre-1870 Poor Law provision for those not already from favoured backgrounds. Anything militating more strongly against a true Conservative philosophy it is difficult to imagine.

If proponents of the voucher scheme are concerned merely to improve choice within the maintained system of education, it is difficult to see why the voucher scheme is *necessary* for this purpose. For it is open to any enlightened local Education Authority to insist that parents be issued with a list of schools within the authority, and asked to record their preferences.

The problem, of course, is to ensure that Education Authorities act in an enlightened way. It is at this point that the second method of strengthening the rights of parents becomes of importance. This involves changes in the law so that, in the interpretation of Section 76 of the Education Act, the onus is shifted away from the parent and on to the local education authority. In other words, instead of the parent having to prove that the authority did not 'have regard to the general principle that . . . pupils are to be educated in accordance with the wishes of their parents' — something which it must, in the nature of things, be difficult to prove — the authority would have to prove that parental wishes could not be satisfied without unreasonable public expenditure, or that the satisfaction of parental wishes would be inconsistent with the provision of efficient instruction and training.

At the same time, there should be an effective appeals system for aggrieved parents. At present, given the broad proviso of Section 76, parents have no real right of appeal against a local authority: it is very rare for the Secretary of State to be able to say that the local education authority acted 'unreasonably'; and in any case, the decision is made within the DES, privately and without reasons being given for the decision.

A system of appeal, therefore, is needed, independent both of the DES and of local education authorities. Local appeals tribunals should be set up within each education authority in order to hear appeals by parents against decisions of the authority. The tribunal would thus be independent, yet not totally divorced from the local education authority. Such tribunals, by adopting standardised methods and giving reasons for their decisions, could build up a body of case law, which would place parents' rights upon a clear and certain footing.

Within this Parents' Charter, a legal framework for the exercise of parental rights, local authority administration of education would become more assured, since it would be founded on a basis of fairness, and parental irritation with educational bureaucracy would be lessened. There is then, at bottom, no real contradiction in supporting local autonomy while demanding that parental rights be guaranteed by law. For local authorities badly need parental involvement and support, if they are successfully to resist central encroachment.

Within this new structure of parental rights and local autonomy, it might be possible to move towards a consensus on the vexed problem of secondary education. There can be no doubt that great harm is done in educational politics and industrial policy by the system of 'adversary politics' whereby each new administration reverses the decision of its political opponents. Parents and teachers alike demand a period of stability during which institutional changes can be absorbed and consolidated. Schools are naturally unwilling to have their status changed with every change of government. To use schools as political shuttlecocks, as the Labour Party has frequently done, is hardly to provide an atmosphere in which quality can flourish.

Unpalatable though it must be to many Conservatives, it must probably be accepted that the decision to end selection at 11 has already been effectively taken by the present Labour Government. By the time the next Conservative Government takes office, the old tripartite system will be dead and comprehensive schools will be established in all authorities. It is unrealistic to expect that newly created comprehensive schools can be unscrambled without severe damage to the morale of teachers and parents who will be committed to making the new system work; and, in any case, supporters of selection, such as the present writer, have long abandoned the idea that the 11-plus represents the most acceptable form of selection. It would, therefore, be difficult to return to the old tripartite system.

No Conservative, however, is likely to be able to support the all-in neighbourhood comprehensive school. The movement towards all-in comprehensive education is hardly likely to lead to any improvement in standards. It represents, indeed, the last fling of the egalitarian consensus of the 1960s. But perhaps even more important is the degree of unfairness which the neighbourhood school will create. Many parents are now becoming familiar with the house agent's advertisement which includes details of catchment areas; in the United States the mean reading scores of the local schools are also included on occasion! Selection by neighbourhood, surely, is far more unfair than anything generated by the 11-plus. Indeed, there is little conviction except among Labour Party stalwarts that the move towards a fully comprehensive system will do any good. Mr

Stuart Maclure, the editor of the *Times Educational Supplement*, writing in that journal on the American experience of comprehensive education [18 April 1975] begins by quoting the following refrain which, he says, 'greets every English educational visitor to North America just now'.

> Do you seriously mean to say that Britain is on the point of getting rid of those first rate grammar schools? Why don't your politicians take the elementary trouble to learn from our mistakes in what has happened to the high school?

Mr Maclure then goes on to say:

> If we simply go ahead on the lines of Circular 10/65 and Circular 4/74, then the grammar school lobby is probably right in saying we shall end up with something like the American answer and many of their complaints.
>
> There is good evidence that the full, unadulterated comprehensive gospel is not held by many in the educational world and by few except ardent party ideologists anywhere.

Lord Alexander, Secretary of the Association of Education Committees, has endorsed this view in opposing the Labour Government's Education Bill.

> I would myself prefer an inquiry into how comprehensive schools should be organised to try to secure that they will be successful and particularly that they will be able to provide for the full range of ability, including children with intellectual gifts — just as provision is made for those with gifts in music or ballet. [*Education*, 2 January 1976]

Is it possible, then, for the Conservative Party to steer a 'Middle Way' between defending a tripartite system that may be irretrievably lost, and supporting a new system which is unlikely to work well, and which in any case involves serious injustice to those children living in less favoured areas?

One possibility, put forward by Mr Maclure, might be for the next Conservative Government to accept the abolition of selection at 11-plus, but ensure that flexibility remains at the 14-plus level. The Labour Government's legislation would be accepted only in so far as it prohibits selection until the age of 14. Beyond that age, selection would be legal. There would then be all-in comprehensive middle schools. These would be smaller than 11–18 comprehensive schools, and therefore many of the difficulties associated with the *size* of comprehensives would be alleviated. At the same time, the 14-plus solution would be more likely than the all-in comprehensive scheme to fit in with existing buildings. This would tend to avoid the problem of the split-site comprehensive.

The post-14 solution would be based on a system of guided parental choice, between courses rather than by examination as in the old 11-plus. This would preserve the advantage of choice, without the central defect of the 11-plus, the public branding of at least three-quarters of every age group as failures at the age of eleven. The 14-plus would thus be a screen and not a barrier. There should be ample opportunity for transfer between courses so as to keep open opportunities for late developers and to allow pupils to postpone critical and irreversible educational decisions for as long as possible.

Local autonomy would also be restored by the scheme, for in place of the imposition of a solution from the centre as in the Labour Government's Education Bill, different authorities could choose their own post-14 solutions; the structure could then evolve in accordance with local initiative.

The grammar schools, direct grant and independent schools would be able to form a satisfactory relationship with the comprehensives, as 14-plus institutions. In this way the direct grant and independent schools could prove to their severest critics that they could contribute effectively to the maintained system, instead of being pushed into the isolation prepared for them by the Labour Government.

But it would also be possible to provide a better deal for the less able and for those who do not wish to pursue their education beyond the school leaving age. These pupils could pursue genuine technical or pre-vocational courses without sacrificing basic literacy or numeracy. What such an education might be like is discussed in the final section of this chapter.

It should, however, already be clear that the 14-plus solution could finally put paid to the Schools Council's harmful and desperate search for a common examination at 16, one replacing the present CSE and GCE 'O' level examinations, but which would neither stretch the able nor provide a genuine incentive for the less able. Those who wished to go on to further education would take 'O' levels or CSE as now; others could be freed from the examination strait-jacket and be allowed to pursue their courses up to the age of 16, without needing to take an external examination. This would remove the threat to standards involved in the 'reform' of the examination system.

But above all, the 14-plus scheme could unite many of those concerned with education in a new consensus. It could obtain a wide measure of support from parents, teachers, teachers' unions and educationalists in general. The scheme could almost certainly be implemented by the next Conservative Government. It would be a practical resolution of a serious educational problem, and should, therefore, appeal to the Conservative Party, which is essentially a practical party concerned with consolidating an existing system and improving upon it, rather than destroying or undermining it in the interests of ideology.

One particular area where the new consensus would yield great benefits is in the education of less able children. It is a chastening thought that 90 per cent of educational discussion makes no reference to the vast majority of the population who lack academic aims; for them the rhetoric of educationalists remains in a stratosphere, light-years away from the pressures and stresses of their daily lives. It is now fifteen years since Mr David Holbrook wrote:

> A good deal of educational comment nowadays – about the social implications of 'streaming', of the 'eleven plus', and about the comprehensive school – seems to assume that differences between children are artificially induced by the needs of our society to maintain an 'elite' on the one hand and a working mass on the other. . . . So much public discourse on education seems irrelevant because the people carrying it on simply do not know the 'low stream' child. [*Guardian*, 28 October 1961, quoted in G. H. Bantock, *Education in an Industrial Society* (2nd ed., 1970).]

After the 1944 Act, there was an almost complete absence of thought concerning the proper role of the secondary modern school which began by apeing the grammar schools, and offering a watered-down grammar school syllabus. Little attention was devoted to either a properly conceived system of pre-vocational education or to education for the satisfactory use of the increasing leisure made possible by the pace of economic and technological advance.

The comprehensive school has, on the whole, failed to remedy this deficiency. The main reason for this is the commitment to the common curriculum and the move towards a common examination system, anything else being held to be unfair or 'divisive'. It is, indeed, frequently overlooked that egalitarianism in education is just as harmful to the less able child as it is to the able. It is time, surely, to free ourselves from this dogma and to realise that the recognition of differences between children requiring different patterns of education is inevitable and necessary. Otherwise, our education system will stand condemned for its failure to provide the average and below-average school leaver with the vocational and cultural resources to enable him to become an intelligent citizen in an industrial and democratic society.

This is not a call for a technical and vocational education in the narrow and crudely utilitarian sense. Indeed, such an education would do more harm than good by predetermining job decisions. What is needed, however, is the designing of courses which allow particular vocational abilities to emerge early, so that pupils can become aware of their real abilities. We might then be able to think seriously about different curricula based upon different aptitudes and capacities, without getting involved in the stultifying argument about which courses were 'superior' or 'inferior'. Ideally, a post-14 system with a wide variety of courses would be well suited to achieve this aim, provided that there was easy transference between different courses for different aptitudes. Again, it is screens and not barriers that are needed.

This in turn might enable us to provide the less able with attitudes conducive to further education after leaving school. Such further education does not by any means necessarily imply a course in a college of further education, but rather a regular resumption of education during different phases of a career until retirement. For nothing in our educational practice will appear more surprising to future generations than our assumption that education is a process completed by the age of 16 (or 18, or 21), with the consequence that adult education and the development of in-service training are treated as the Cinderellas of the education service.

For in the advanced technological society in which we live, continual adaptation to new skills will be necessary for almost everyone throughout their working lives. In the words of a Canadian Commission set up to study the problem of acquiring new skills:

> Increasingly we accept the fact that traditional schooling – formal learning throughout a set period of childhood and early adult years – can no longer see most of us confidently through the rest of our lives. . . . [*The Learning Society*, Report of the Commission on Postsecondary Education (Ontario, 1972).]

We need, then, to concern ourselves about the notion of recurrent education (*éducation permanente*) and about the forms it might take in Britain. But the first step clearly is to motivate pupils to an appreciation of the fact that their education cannot end on the day they leave school.

Unfortunately, the raising of the school-leaving age was, from this point of view, a retrograde step, since it tends to increase rather than to overcome resistance to education. Instead of a longer period of initial education, what is needed is to convey to pupils the need to withdraw from their work at different phases of their career in order to acquire new skills. It has been rightly said that:

> Many of the future problems of adult reluctance or inability to learn might be solved if today's young worker could build continued learning so fully into his habit pattern that he took it for granted. [Dr E. and Dr R. M. Belbin, quoted in F. Jessup (ed.), *Lifelong Learning*]

This task of course requires close co-operation between teachers, schools and industry. Industry itself has perhaps most to gain from an enlightened approach to recurrent education. For, if working people know that the threat of unemployment as a result of technical change can be replaced by the acquisition of new skills, then surely much of the 'Luddite' attitude to overmanning which so bedevils British industry would disappear; and industry can only benefit from the discovery of new potentialities amongst its work force.

For the Conservative Party support for recurrent education should be part of a wider programme for the humanising of work relationships. Nothing could be more important for industrial policy, and therefore for economic progress, than to discover and eliminate the causes of alienation at work. If the Conservative Party is to be committed to a socially responsible capitalism, it must understand that the causes of our industrial failure lie not only in economic mistakes, but also in our radically defective view of education.

It is impossible to calculate to what extent industrial troubles are caused by a feeling of alienation from work, a feeling that the work relationship is devoid of dignity instead of being, as it should be, something that expresses and satisfies human needs. Ernst Cassirer in his *Essay on Man* argued that work was 'the system of human activities which defines and determines the circle of humanity', for men need to know that they are rendering some useful service to the society in which they live. But the humanising of industrial society requires not only the reform of work relationships, but also a parallel reform of the education system, so that education comes to be considered in the broadest sense as a preparation for work and for leisure. At this point, education policy links hands with industrial policy, and education becomes, as the Victorians well understood, a central force in the revival of our national fortunes.

These themes, then — the maximum degree of local initiative in decision-making compatible with the maintenance of national standards and the rights of parents; the creation of a new consensus in secondary education; and the adoption of a programme of recurrent education — should provide the foundation of Conservative education policy. They imply a society efficient yet humane — a decentralised society restoring choice and opportunity, yet preserving quality. It is the kind of society in which the vast majority of British people would like to live.

10 Conservatism and Science

GRAHAM RICHARDS

Just as it is a myth that science has nothing to say about religion it is equally untrue that science is apolitical. Throughout most of its history science has been a revolutionary subject with a definite left-wing flavour and yet it has provided increasing personal freedom. The last decade has witnessed a dramatic change of emphasis: science is becoming progressively more conservative and there are real fears about the effects of science on freedom.

Science is not a single subject, but a spectrum, ranging from physics at one end to biological science at the other. The change in the attitudes of science results from the swing of emphasis from physical science towards the life sciences. This change has not yet been seen as a qualitative transformation which alters the relationship between science and politics, perhaps because most philosophers of science are still preoccupied with physics. None the less, it is clearly the case that science seems to be in the course of changing sides in the political debate.

Throughout the five hundred years or so of the modern period, science has been a revolutionary subject rather than an evolutionary discipline. The revolutions have been swift and dramatic, altering history in a quite discontinuous manner. Agriculture gave way to industry; travel became possible for the masses; diseases which had held men in check for millenia disappeared; and contraceptive pills did more for women's liberation than any legislation. Science more than politics has transformed the face of the earth and the life-style in scientifically sophisticated societies. As a result, science was confident of its strength and undoubting in its belief that all the problems of man, both realised and still to come, would fall to man's own ingenuity in the form of scientific advance. This self-confidence has now evaporated and most scientists view the future as a period when we will not be providing new miracles to alter the way of life of our species, but rather as an era when we will be increasingly concerned with protecting what has already been achieved and minimising the harmful effects of previous revolutions.

Many observers of the current scene see the oil crisis as an historical watershed. Some things will never be the same again. Viewed from the vantage point of science this crisis seems to be a sympton rather than a cause. It is only one manifestation of an increasingly obvious limitation on future development brought on by the finite limit on resources and an increasing awareness of the effects of change on the rest of our system.

This awareness receives its most clear-cut expression in the rise of conservation societies and the increasing use of ecological arguments. The gradual influence of such ideas stems from the change of the centre of gravity of science away from physical science. It is the rise of biology and its kindred subjects as the most exciting and prestigious source of problems that has altered the emphasis of science from revolution to conservatism.

Any study of biology forces attention towards the interrelation of the different parts of a whole system. If the physicist produces a device which will lead to television, then the sociological changes which the revolutionary invention will produce are scarcely debated. Problems are only considered when they arise and are thought to be very much of secondary importance. In biology it is quite different. Any innovation is likely to lead to numerous complications since once one upsets any part of a network of delicately balanced equilibria the ramifications are likely to be felt all through the system. As a result the science of ecology has become so fashionable and, for example, manufacturers of pesticides must take inordinate trouble to avoid unwanted effects in their products. The very nature of biology then leads to a desire to protect what is worth protecting and included in this is the *status quo*. This is the essence of conservatism.

It is not even too fanciful to point out that whereas physical science has very few women practitioners at the highest level, biological science seems to attract able women, who have an innate feeling for the subject. Either from genetic origins or because of social pressure, it is also true that women have a tendency, albeit with obvious exceptions, towards the conservation of life and the protection of the environment.

Although science is becoming conservative due to the rise of biology the process is far from complete. Physics remains a revolutionary rather than evolutionary subject and in many areas the two philosophies compete.

Highlighted by the oil crisis precipitated by the Middle East war is our current energy problem. It has been taxing the scientific community for some time. Here is a perfect example of the dichotomy between the approach of physics and that of biology. To the physicist the short-term solution is nuclear fission, and the long-term panacea is unlimited power from nuclear fusion using cheap lithium or even seawater. Despite the fact that the physicist is aware that fission reactions will cause an increase in the background radioactive radiation and an atomic waste problem which will remain for tens of thousands of years, to say nothing of possible accidents, he is keen to persist. With hundreds of millions of pounds being spent on fusion research they scarcely even question whether unlimited cheap power would be desirable. So long as crude calculations reassure the experimenters that the earth's weather will not be drastically altered then the research continues.

The biological approach to the same problem is quite different. The starting point is the consideration that the earth receives from the sun sufficient energy for all its needs in the foreseeable future providing it can be harnessed. The line of thought is to use plants, or tides, or man-made systems which maximise certain biological techniques, in order to harness solar energy. In this way it is hoped that the minimum upset of the balance of nature will result.

If a totally conservative policy were to be adopted then it might seem that man ought to do nothing other than accept what he receives. However, man himself is part of the environment and it is our nature to innovate. The biological approach is to ensure that our artificial changes do not upset the system too much and that any change will, if possible, preserve the desired aspects of life while reducing or eliminating unwanted features. Because the biologist is aware of the infinite complexity of life, he is fearful of introducing large changes because of the unknown results of his tampering. The revolutionary physicist has no such qualms and reassures himself with the fact that most of his major steps have in the past been beneficial.

Research on nuclear problems has very rarely been criticised or even questioned by the physicists actually involved. In biology the risks in a particular research programme are much more likely to be explored. Recently there has been a striking example. A conference was held at Asilomer in California to discuss limitations on research in what is popularly described as genetic engineering. Although at such a level there is a suggestion that big names in the field are trying to produce restrictions which mean that only they may pursue the study and despite the fact that some of the potentially most dangerous experiments were performed almost five years ago, none the less, the very fact that such a discussion took place and guidelines have been produced by committees of eminent men indicates a new conservatism of major science.

At the same time as being conservative this new mood of science is also anti-establishment and anti-monopoly. Attitudes common among bio-logists, but also becoming known among physical scientists, are not welcome in totalitarian environments either behind the iron curtain or in huge multinational companies. The new conservative scientist is much more likely to question the use of animals in research or the value of the end-product than the traditional boffin in a white coat.

This leads to perhaps the most curious feature of the new conservatism. It is not welcomed by people who would call themselves Conservatives politically and the young caring conservative scientists are emotionally and practically more likely to be of the left. We are then left with the curious phenomenon that groups such as the Friends of the Earth are considered as left-wing bodies even though their aims are not just conservationist, but Conservative.

The denial of conservatism by Conservatives has much in common with the denial of socialism by many so-called Socialists. The aims of trades unions can scarcely be called socialist when, despite the mouthings of their leaders, the weight of their efforts are directed towards increased pay packets with scant regard for any other section of society, even for the poor. The Conservative party seems in the public mind over-tied financially to big business,and committed to economic growth at any price, so that the multinational company is succoured even if its policies are anything but conservative.

Politics and sociology are closely related to biology and surely have something to learn from the scientific and philosophical discoveries in the life sciences. It is now abundantly clear that many well-meant 'improvements' in life, although initially and superficially regarded as triumphs, have more recently been considered as disasters. The use of revolutionary drugs or pesticides, of new crops or of new materials have in countless instances brought immediate apparent benefit, but long-term disaster. This fact is now so imprinted on the scientific conscience that we hesitate to kill off an apparent pest lest in our ignorance it plays some part in a vital set of interconnected relations which would be disturbed by too severe a perturbation of the system.

If biology is complex, how much more so is human life? Sociological experiments are infinitely more complex than the biological ones yet the cautionary wisdom of biology is ignored. Housing, town planning and state participation are treated in the way science used to behave. Drastic changes are introduced; one may cite high-rise flats, comprehensive schools, complete revolutions in taxation. No biologist would behave in this manner even when dealing with a much less complex situation.

Let us suppose that scientists discover a hitherto unknown valley in an extinct volcano in central Africa. The region will first be studied in its natural state much as historians and sociologists study our own society. Certainly the investigation of the valley will find distressing signs of nature's cruelty: big animals will prey on the weak; insects may make life unbearable for some species; grazing animals will eat pasture which contains beautiful and delicate plants. In former times the intruding scientist might shoot some of the big game, use DDT on the insects or fence out the animals. The mood of current science is to adopt a humble attitude which would question most such actions and probably result in most obvious steps being avoided because of the realisation that time and evolutionary forces have probably resulted in the optimum equilibrium for the ultimately restricting conditions of physical and chemical limitations.

It is too facile and obviously over-simple to treat the world in which we take part in a manner precisely analogous to the newly discovered biological environment. We are part of the environment and must play our own role, not that of gods. If total *laissez-faire* were to reign then no progress would have been made in so many areas: we would not have tried to eliminate pathogenic bacteria, crippling diseases, urban squalor or physical discomfort. On the other hand, our lives are conducted in a biological environment so that some of the self-imposed restraints adopted by the ecologist should be applied to political activity.

In medicine the awareness of problems created by solving other problems is apparent. Are we justified in saving victims of thrombosis if we only condemn them to miserable incapacitated senility? Most of us worry that medical science may keep us alive after some disaster when, were we to have had the choice, we would prefer to have perished. The ethical problems of medicine do exercise the minds of doctors, but the precisely similar problems created by political acts are frequently ignored.

Revolutionary and left-wing parties are more at fault in making violent change than are conservatives who do prefer to evolve, but at the same time there are areas where Conservatives fail to conserve. It is not the Conservative Party which has the reputation for removing traffic from city centres, putting freight on to the railways or preventing suburban sprawl. In many instances the Conservative Party has acted more as the representative of business than as the party with a sound ecological philosophy. Rather worse, during the years of power, 1970 to 1974, the Conservatives acquired the image not just of being the friends of big business, but of being the friends of the developer who cared least for any conservation policy. The resultant over-reaction has produced the catastrophic Community Land Act, amongst others.

Science in its newly emerging form can thus suggest a course of behaviour for a political party. The converse is also true. Government largely controls science through funding and must have a policy for science. This is particularly important at the present time because the change of emphasis in science from the physical to the biological has worrying consequences as well as the encouraging ecological and conservationist aspects.

The chief worry to a conservative must be the influence of science on freedom. In the past science has been a provider of freedom: freedom from disease, from hunger, from geographical restriction. It has been a provider of information and communication systems with radio, television and rapid transportation vehicles. The very success of science in these areas is now bringing poblems, both at the macroscopic and at the microscopic levels. The macroscopic effect is the obvious though terrifying population explosion. The microscopic is less familar and less understandable to the layman. It is not an exaggeration to say that the potential power of biologists to alter man's own hereditary material by genetic engineering is more frightening and potentially more dramatic in its ramifications than was the work of physicists in uncovering the power in the atomic nucleus.

Very fortunately, biologists are inevitably conservative and conscious of the potential dangers in a way which revolutionary naive physicists were not. However, despite their conservatism the power now exists in the hands of scientists to transform personal freedom or even the freedom of our whole species.

Some glimmering of the possibilities of the future can be seen in the current dilemmas of medical ethics. The effect on the population of the future in keeping alive people who in natural circumstances would not have survived is to alter significantly the genetic make-up of the future generations. This problem already faces workers in medical research, but how much more difficult it will be if we actually alter the genetic material rather than merely allow defective strains to survive.

Science can alter the whole nature of future populations, of future crops, of future forms of habitation, possibly even of future weather. Many of the decisions must be political. In the wrong political hands terrifying inroads on personal freedom become possible, including changing future populations much more radically than Hitler's attempts at eugenics. Science is becoming aware of these problems and so too must politicians, who normally think on too short a time-scale for any long-term effects to be apparent.

Knowledge brings problems; problems which governments must control. It is clear that the nature of these difficulties demands that scientists should be more closely involved in politics rather than just used as advisers. However, the involvement of science in politics itself is not without danger. Already we see democracy threatened because economic arguments are beyond the comprehension of the layman. This is not too serious since the experts disagree and the untutored Member of Parliament or the voter can make his decision on the basis of which expert commands most confidence. With scientific arguments it is less satisfactory. The arguments may be quite outside the capacity of non-experts to judge and there may be no scientific disagreement. To a very large extent this was true of the decisions both to build and to use the atomic bomb. There are areas where the scientist is far more than an adviser; he really takes the decision, but does not have the responsibility of an elected politician. We are thus presented with the possibility that knowledge of the governmental process will come to be limited to those who can not only master the technical vocabulary, but also really understand the science. The only long-term solution would seem to be more involvement of scientists in politics and more scientific education for the public.

The short-term problem of science which now faces governments is to have a science policy at a time when much of science is growing ever more costly and at the same time less obviously useful. Recent attempts to come some way towards dealing with this problem include the Rothschild report. In this and a number of similar governmental and commercial policy statements the essential thesis is that if government is to pay vast sums for research then it has a right to expect that the recipients will work towards some practical useful ends.

This view does not provide a programme of science policy for a future Conservative Government if one adopts the approach taken in this chapter that science is becoming more and more conservative, with a swing towards biology. For science is an activity of civilised man just like music or the arts. At this level science deserves support as a cultivating influence and the financial support should go to the able individual rather than the project. This surely should appeal to Conservative policy makers. When the costs are not enormous it is the individual who should get support and not the institution.

Certain areas of big science on the other hand demand an entrance fee so high that it is unrealistic to favour personalities. In these big-spending fields successive Governments have been duped by powerful groups of scientists seeking support for pet prestigious schemes when the only people capable of judging the ideas were direct or indirect beneficiaries. Conservative Governments could save vast sums of money, not by taking a mean Treasury attitude, but rather by making decisions based on Conservative principles. When considering Concorde the wide range of probable effects should be taken into account; not merely the effect on the ozone layer or on the voters of outer London, but on the world at large, if it is presented with very fast travel. That is a relatively easy example where the beneficial and harmful changes may be finely balanced. On the other hand the nuclear power decisions could be made more rationally than they are at present if the preoccupations of current science become the preoccupations of politicians.

The new preoccupations of science are, then: the preservation of things which must be preserved; the notion that any change must be gradual enough not to disturb any related equilibria, and the problem of freedom of the individual weighted against the needs of our species. These are precisely the preoccupations of the Conservative Party, too.

11 Industrial Relations

LORD GOWRIE

The main obstacle in the way of a Conservative return to power is a gut feeling by ordinary voters that Conservatives would not be able to handle industrial relations. Nearly all surveys of popular opinion show that people believe that Labour knows how to 'get on with the unions'; yet paradoxically the unions at the same time are usually held to blame for the steadily worsening British economy, not least by members of trade unions themselves. Even if currency collapse or a sharp increase in unemployment were to bring the Labour Government down, most people suspect that the incoming Conservatives would find union consent denied them, or confrontation with the unions forced upon them. Thus indeed the most urgent political problem facing the Party in the next decade, whether in office or opposition, is not only how to appear, but how to be credible in handling industrial relations and dealing generally with trade unions as the most powerful group in the modern industrial state.

At the same time, bleak economic circumstances and poor prospects for Great Britain make it likely that a Conservative Government will be returned sooner or later. When Harold Wilson resigned in March 1976 the pound was worth 36p in relation to its value when he first became Prime Minster in 1964. About a third of this depreciation took place in the two years since he succeeded Edward Heath in 1974. Unemployment, at 1⅓ million, stood higher than at any time since 1947 and this in the first stage – the £6 pay limit – of a wages and prices policy. The electoral prospects of Labour depend on a lucky combination of events: that the upturn of the advanced economies of the world, coupled with the downturn of the pound, will get British exports under way before increased import costs bring the bandwagon to a halt once again; that the anomalies created by Stages One and Two of Labour's pay policy do not prove fatal to Stage Three; that Scotland will postpone secession during a time of Royal Jubilee; that Mr Callaghan will an enjoy an Indian summer of electoral esteem. Nevertheless the best shot in the Labour locker will surely remain a general suspicion, shared by a number of Conservatives, that trade unions will not co-operate with Mrs Thatcher. Well played, and the Labour leadership is skilful and experienced, this response could be turned into a self-fulfilling prophecy. But even if Labour luck holds, and the conditions are fulfilled, the problems of prolonged wage control will in the end bring the Tories back to power, and thus to their industrial relations dilemma.

This chapter, accordingly, will attempt two things. One is to argue that Britain need not be ungovernable, in the sense that a democratically elected Government can conduct a programme which the leadership of the more powerful unions dislikes for political reasons. I use the phrases 'need not be ungovernable' and 'can conduct a programme' because built into this argument is the qualification that such a Government may have to deny itself control of prices and incomes as an instrument of policy. The second aim is to demonstrate that while there does exist a threat to the survival of our democratic institutions, it comes less from the unions than from the tendency of all governments to offer the electorate a number of irreconcilable alternatives simulataneously: stable prices; full employment; a steady rise in consumption; ever-increasing welfare benefits; significant personal liberties. So long as governments, and I have to include Conservative Governments, go on trying to square the circle, our economy will be in danger of collapse. Collapse will not simply involve a change of administration or leadership, a period of belt-tightening or dusting down of the Dunkirk spirit. It will put an end, for the rest of the century at least, to the relative improvement which our time has made to mass living standards and expectations. It is hard to see how the kind of personal choices and democratic freedoms we enjoy could stand an immediate and permanent (so far as our own lifetimes are concerned) reduction, to some quarter or half of present levels, of the standards of workpeople's life in this country. We would be in the position of East Germany, say, in 1950; and with rather worse prospects. We would survive, because we are a tenacious and talented people and because we have natural resources. Those of us who put equality above all other aims would see their wishes fulfilled. The suddenness and sharpness of the shock might even make us 'great' again. But we would not survive in what we presently interpret as a democracy.

There is not a shred of evidence to show that the unionised work force of this country wants this to happen. There is a great deal of evidence to the contrary. About half the working population of Britain is unionised; about a third of the unionised workers vote Tory and a slightly higher percentage of non-unionised workers do so as well. A Conservative programme which can clearly identify what has gone wrong with the national economy, in which all workers have the principal interest, will increase its level of worker support. A Conservative programme which also can open up opportunities of improvement will not obtain consent merely, and thereby quell a temporary political embarrassment. It will command massive support and co-operation. The industrial relations dilemma, therefore, is little different from the national dilemma; the Tory task from the national task.

Perhaps the first task for Conservatives is to clear away popular misconceptions about trade union power. In fairness, many such misconceptions stem from Conservatives themselves, or from the trauma the party suffered when Mr Heath's Government fell in March 1974. The Conservatives fought an election, expecting to win it, sixteen months before term. They did so against a background of the almost total failure of their industrial policy. In 1970 they had promised the electorate to trim state powers of intervention in industry; to halt inflation, which ordinary people saw in terms of rising prices, especially food prices; to make trade union practices and the conduct of industrial relations accountable in law; and to release the economic energies of the British people, easing credit restrictions and lowering taxes, in order to coax the country towards a rate of growth closer to the European average. By 1974 the Industry Act, the most interventionist piece of legislation passed by Parliament up to that time, was on the statute book; the rate of *domestic* inflation had, indeed, been slowed down but only relative to its being previously accelerated by the Government in pursuit of growth and at the cost of reversing an election commitment to abandon legal controls over prices and wages. The Industrial Relations Act, which arrived on the statute book after exhausting Parliamentary struggles and considerable union disruption outside, underwent effective boycott from employers as well as from unions. The money which the Chancellor, Mr Barber, released into public hands found its way into consumer spending and the service and property sectors rather than into industry. Industry itself was on three-day working. The wonder was not so much that the Conservatives lost the general election, but that, as in 1964, they nearly won it — achieving, indeed, a somewhat larger share of the popular vote than that obtained by the Labour Party.

Mr Heath had gone to the country with the clear question: who rules Britain? — a government drawn from elected representatives or trade unions accountable only to their own membership? He received an altogether confused answer. Mr Wilson's minority government came to power. Within a year the State was in control of more sectors of the national economy than ever before; inflation was nudging 30 per cent; the Government's decisions were, by their own admission, effectively taken by the leaders of organised labour, many age-old individual rights being legally subsumed by collectivist ones; the country was more deeply in debt than at any period in its history and its industrial output, which had risen by 7½ per cent during the three-and-a-half years of Conservative government, was now in fact nil. To add insult to injury, Harold Wilson beat the Tories by 40 odd seats in the general election of October 1974, who in February 1975 took the unprecedented step of voting out their leader. Small wonder then, that the average Conservative supporter, in Parliament or outside it, feared the powers of organised labour and suggested a policy vacuum where industrial relations were concerned.

The reality, however, was not so simple. It was not just that the unions had taken on the Conservatives and won. That was no more true than the belief that the Heath Government's Industrial Relations Act, which sought only to bring Britain's industrial practices in line with those of her more successful competitors, was an assault on the rights and protections of individual workers. The Act was of course nothing of the kind; it was an attempt, foreshadowed in principle and in many points of detail by the previous Labour Government's White Paper *In Place of Strife*, to deal with an uncomfortable, and to the general public largely unknown, set of facts concerning British trade unionism. Foremost is the complexity of our union structure. We have a work force of 24 million people, about half of whom are unionised. These are represented by more than *three hundred* unions and fewer than half again affiliated to the TUC.

The origins of such proliferation lie in our history as the first nation state to industrialise on any scale and need not concern us here. The effects concern us very much indeed, and contribute hugely to outsiders' view that Britain has the worst, in the sense of least 'bankable' or reliable, system of industrial bargaining in the world.

Consider just one example. At the time this essay was being written (in spring 1976) a damaging unofficial strike had just finished in a Birmingham carburettor plant, halting production of carburettors for more than 95 per cent of British Leyland vehicles. The strike was not directed at the company (now, of course, in effect a nationalised industry) since the toolmen involved were asking for parity with toolmen in other non-Leyland plants. The Leyland management would have granted the increase but for the Government's £6 'voluntary' incomes policy, the toolmen having already had their increase within the then wage round. Meantime, at the Standard-Triumph complex near Coventry, a strike by 350 toolmakers had stopped production of all Stag, TR6, Dolomite and Spitfire cars. In this case, the *toolmakers* complained that their differentials over *production* workers had been compressed by the pay policy and they wanted parity with the *tinsmiths,* the highest-paid *craft* group. Meantime again, back at the Rover-Triumph division of British Leyland, a third group of strikers stopped production of the Land-Rover and Range-Rover vehicles and necessitated 4000 lay-offs. This dispute was over the exact interpretation of an existing pay agreement: that is to say, of something already agreed. All these strikes had been opposed by Mr Hugh Scanlon, of the Engineers; but he had also pointed out that even with 17,000 workers idle in the group the pressure to restore differentials could not be contained indefinitely after their return.

By the time this book is read, the disputes in question will no doubt be long forgotten: all of them swelling the dismal statistic that about 90 per cent of strikes are unofficial and not, therefore, easy to settle on a management/union or even Government/union basis. Nor are advance agreements much use in British industrial relations. They make Continental and American wage bargaining enviable. Not only do the two sides of industry there meet across one table, but lawyers are present as well. The instance given, or rather the set of instances within a given industry, shows up the competitive and localised nature of British industrial disputes. It shows, too, the difficulties which governments may encounter if they try to run a wage control policy for longer than a year or two, or if they try to achieve 'fairness' as well as help for the lower paid by giving everyone the same rate of increase.

Such difficulties obtain whichever government is in power. If we look at them carefully we will, I believe, come to the conclusion that central control of prices and incomes is an instrument of economic management which Conservatives especially should use only *in extremis*: that is, if the rate of unemployment is appreciably higher than the highest level achieved by the previous Labour Government. It is still a tempting instrument to many Conservatives. This is partly because Mr Heath's Stage One and Stage Two were successful: Britain in 1972 and 1973 had the second lowest rate of inflation in the West. (What a contrast to Mr Healey's claims of success for Labour's wage policy — with Britain in 1976 suffering the second highest.) It is also a tempting instrument because, as we have seen, many people look upon wage controls as a last chance to integrate the trade unions within the overall management of our economy, break down the 'us and them' confrontation system, and spike the guns of militancy and the extreme left once and for all. Both Mr Heath and Mr Benn are alike in favouring the kind of corporatism that would formally affiliate the trade union movement to the administrative machinery of the state. But tempting as a permanent wages policy may appear, it nevertheless remains a chimera. Workers of all kinds are at least as interested in differentials and special rewards for special skills as in what TUC rhetoric calls 'fair shares'. We have, too, the evidence of the referendum on Europe, as well as of all Conservative electoral victories, to show that the political aims of union leaders are very often at odds with those of their rank and file. It should not be part of Conservative industrial relations policy to *politicise* the trade union movement further. We know from experience that a wages policy has special dangers for the Tories, since for political rewards in the short term, and no economic rewards in the long term, it brings the leadership of a party opposed by Labour in Parliament into direct confrontation with the leadership of the labour movement in industry.

At a time of world inflation, when prices are rising outside the country for reasons over which governments have little or no control, there is much to be said for controlling wages so that they will not immediately respond to existing price rises, anticipate future ones, or guarantee a substantial addition to both by passing on the response in higher wage claims. An economy like ours, buying more than half its food and raw materials abroad, compounds the trouble by balance of payments difficulties and their effect on our currency. The drawbacks to prices and incomes policies are quite simple: they are democracy and the mixed economy. People do not like them, or rather are in favour of them only in so far as they do not last very long or erode differentials in pay. Business, and private business in particular, cannot long survive control of prices because increased labour costs may not be passed on to the consumer, profits are squeezed, and interest levels remain high enough to drown the possibility of investment. The alternative to bankruptcy becomes dependency on government, since government may still have opportunities for borrowing denied to the individual enterprise. Government has access, too, to the printing press.

Nor do union leaders like wage controls. Their principal function, the function of unionism in general, is to *bargain* pay increases for their members. (One of the nails in the Heath Government's coffin was Sir Derek Ezra's positively oriental wiliness in handing over all that the Coal Board were able to offer in one lump, thereby undermining Mr Joe Gormley's role as a negotiator.) This is notwithstanding that a long-term policy of wages and prices control is a recipe for a fully socialised state. One of the vanquishers of Mr Heath in 1974, the coalmen's Mr Arthur Scargill, is quite aware of this and has argued that it is wrong for a Labour Government (i.e. a social democratic government) to impose wage control in order to prop up a mixed economy; wage control must be a socialist, not a capitalist weapon. Interviewed in September 1975 he said:

> On television recently we had the remarkable spectacle of three union leaders saying, 'We want to operate the social contract to help keep the Labour Party in and not the Tories.' In other words, we want the Labour Government to impose a wage freeze after we've thrown out the Tories for imposing a wage freeze. What a contradiction!
>
> We now have a Labour Government that is deliberately operating measures that are designed to solve the capitalist crisis at the expense of the workers. I'm not prepared to pay for the crisis of capitalism at the expense of the people I represent . . . The only way we'd all put it right is if we all control everything in our society.

One need not share Mr Scargill's politics to find this acute. A *permanent* prices and incomes policy is exactly what Conservatives are in politics to avoid. It is at least worth noticing that it is also what most trade union leaders are in office to avoid.

The shifts in governmental thinking over centralised control of wages are notorious. It might be kinder to say the shifts imposed on governmental thinking by events; but we must also remember that the events which lead to incomes policies are sometimes of governments' own making. Mr Wilson was pro in Government, anti in opposition, pro again in Government. This progress perfectly mirrors his European approaches and must, of course, be an instance of the political skill for which he is so often congratulated. Mr Heath was anti in opposition, and anti in Government – that is until Lord Rothschild and Sir William Armstrong persuaded him that wage restraint might enable him to continue to aim for growth in the economy while cutting the level of unemployment (about half Mr Wilson's legacy to Mr Callaghan) which public-sector wage inflation, following the settlement of the miners' first strike early in 1972, was driving irresistibly upward. Indeed employment rates were the spur. Conservative Governments care more about high levels of unemployment than Labour Governments; partly because they are politically vulnerable to Labour Party and trade union collusion on the issue and partly because their tradition is directed toward self-reliance and self-support. Mr Heath tried for voluntary agreement with the union high command. The Industrial Relations Act denied it him so he imposed statutory controls, somewhat along Mr Nixon's lines, with astonishing success between November 1972 and November 1973.

Unfortunately, this success continues to haunt Tory thinking. The policy appeared to have been brought down more by bad luck than bad judgement. Import prices continued to rise beyond anyone's calculations. Russian agricultural failure sent cereals, and therefore animal feedstuffs, through the roof. Since Mr Heath was widely believed to have achieved his surprise victory in 1970 through the housewives' 'foodbasket' vote this damaged him personally with electorate. The world energy crisis imposed by OPEC strengthened the miners' hand at the same time as it weakened the Government's; a market-oriented or 'Selsdon' administration might have latched on to this correspondence. The Government read the miniscule drop in production after three-day working was imposed as an indication that workers everywhere resented the miners' obduracy, especially as the money on offer was bigger than average and Stage Three of the Counter-Inflation Policy had been drawn up with the miners in mind. This reading was substantially correct, showing that there are no inherent reasons why a Conservative Government cannot receive as wide worker support in office as it obtains in order to reach Number Ten. But the Government misread the union high command's genuine desire to get the country back to work; a feeling Mr Wilson and Mr Callaghan skilfully, and quite justifiably, exploited. Nevertheless the Tory working-class vote stood up well in the election and in more normal times (no higher-than-average turnout; no Liberal Party false dawn; no Mr Enoch Powell) a comparable performance would have swept the Government home. The same vote fell heavily in the second general election of the year; ironically because Labour retained the threshold agreements of Mr Heath's Stage Three. These had been designed before the oil price increases were known and in consequence were an inflationary disaster. The unemployed in Britain will pay for their unscrupulous retention by Labour for years to come.

I have dwelt on the 1974 débâcle because it is essential to learn its lessons for the future. The main lesson is that running a wages policy at all is dangerous for governments and especially for Conservative Governments: the Labour Opposition being able to identify directly with those whose wages are under control. Moreover the cosmetics of such policies require price control as well. Nothing is more dangerous to our mixed economy than the oversimplified equating of prices with incomes. Price control and dividend restriction are too high a price to pay for wage restraint since profits are not, as union rhetoric has it and the civil service seems to believe, mere swag for the wealthy. (An examination paper in the subject might ask the following question: 'Discuss the effects of price and dividend restriction between 1972 and 1976 on the financing of trade union activities and responsibilities.') In fact, British workers will 'forgive' the Tories long before the City forgives them. Without profitability there is investment starvation, coronary occlusion of cash flow, paralysis of labour, postponement of expansion and recruitment. The managers of British Rail's pension funds know this very well; they are at present the biggest purchasers of fine art in the world. So much for Mr Benn's colourful accusation that recent years have witnessed a strike by capital.

A wages policy is certainly one method of keeping within bounds the unemployment which rapid depreciation of money always brings. But as Mr Wilson learned in 1967–9, as Mr Heath learned in 1974 and as Mr Jack Jones has known all his life (hence his predilection for flat rate increases), wage policies of any sophistication or durability are incompatible with the fragmentariness and multiplicity of unions in Britain. Using irony, it can be said that before you have wage control you need a workable Industrial Relations Act. One group, or sub-group, or sub-sub-group can all too easily blow the whole edifice apart; clear recognition procedures are of the essence. If a Conservative Government operates the policy, there may be pressure from Labour to back union resistance to control. Even if the high command of the TUC were in agreement (as Mr Scargill felt they were) with the *principle* of restraint, they might well feel that even tacit support of a Conservative Government would undermine union moderates and increase left-wing militancy.

Then there is the illusion that a political programme acceptable to the TUC, or in line with union leaders' thinking, can magically engender wage restraint or nullify opposition to wage controls. The infamous 'social contract' of March 1974 to July 1975, which Mr Wilson actually accused the Tories of envying, sent inflation from 13 to 30 per cent. It did so not because the union leadership were in disagreement with the Government. No Prime Minister in British history has ever been so responsive to a single group in society as Mr Wilson to the trade unions between March 1974 and his resignation two years later. Even the landed classes were not exempted from constitutional obligations in the heyday of property. Rather were the unions using the social contract (son of the 'Solomon Binding' who died in 1965) to re-establish the differentials which Mr Heath's policy had eroded and which the meanest shop steward knew would be stamped on once more by the controls Mr Wilson, or rather his creditors, were soon to impose. Samuel Brittan has made the point well.

> Why should one suppose that the adoption of any target reduction of inequality (however defined), or of the shares of property incomes, would induce greater restraint in union wage claims? The more that policy concentrates on eliminating disparities and differentials, the greater the sense of outrage likely to be engendered by those that remain. Moreover, the smaller the financial contrast between the mass of wage-salary earners and the wealthy minority, the greater the attention that is likely to be paid to relativities among workers. As it is, 90 per cent of consumer spending comes from wages, salaries and welfare payments, and the annual wage round is to a large extent a contest between different groups of workers for relative shares. It is one of the defects, both of formal incomes policy — with its norms, criteria, exceptions, and regulatory Boards — and of an informal 'compact', that each group becomes much more keenly aware of what other groups are obtaining; and this increases rather than diminishes the ferocity of the struggle.

Indeed who can blame union officials for honouring their professional obligations and fighting for the interests of the members who pay them? As the Donovan Report showed ten years ago, the great flaw in British industrial relations is not union power so much as weakness: the weakness engendered by jurisdictional disputes between competing unions in an economy whose low rate of growth is bound to cause overmanning, restrictive practices and other industrial ills. It is a case not just of fighting for a larger share of a shrinking pie, of a pie which you know will contain few plums at next baking, but of clinging fiercely to the piece you were offered in the first place.

Assuming, then, that commitment to a prices and incomes policy is fraught with peril for Conservatives, how would a Conservative Government control inflation? The short answer is that they need vigorously to withstand the key inflationary temptations: deficit financing (spending too much money) and manipulating demand (pumping too much money or credit into the system) so as to reduce short-term unemployment. At this point in the argument a worried agent or party manager is likely to make political noises of objection. The Conservatives will be fighting the next general election on a positive and expansionist platform; the real reduction in living standards through world recession as well as the first fifteen months of the Social Contract will see to that. Would it not be easy for Labour to claim that while their levels of employment were bad, Conservative levels would be worse? (This was deployed to some effect during the Coventry by-election in March 1976.) How too could the Tories reconcile a programme of reduced taxation with a refusal to manipulate demand? Above all, if a Conservative programme were to pick up needed worker support by becoming the party in favour of pay differentials and free collective bargaining, the traditional middle-class voter, suffering much in recent years through lack of collectivist power, would surely find himself clobbered yet again and alienated from the party for ever.

These are not cynical questions, concerned with capturing power merely or selling a political programme. They go to the heart of the national, and therefore the Conservative dilemma. But there is a solution; and it is possible for the Conservatives to construct a platform which refuses to cover up difficulties but which is nevertheless radical and simple in its appeal.

The basic clue is that the post-war Keynesian orthodoxy (using fiscal and monetary levers to create employment by manipulating demand) is breaking down fast. The inflationary consequences are clear both to the centre and right of the Labour party; in fairness to the supporters and admirers of Mr Roy Jenkins as Chancellor in 1968–9 it might be said that they always have been. Until the Labour left obtains real power, in the sense of orchestrating very wide support outside the Parliamentary Party, it will not be easy for members of the present Cabinet, should they find themselves in opposition to Mrs Thatcher, to attack the more balanced Budgets of her Chancellor. It also may be that the public will not permit in other leaders the *volte-faces* they tolerated in Mr Wilson. Something like a new consensus of economic management is in the process of formation; if it is the right one we must see that it coheres. Sacrifices, of course, will have to be made. With unemployment approaching 1½ million, it is tempting for Tory candidates, or members with marginal seats, to bellow for reflation. Instead they should *encourage* the Government to alter in their own, and reality's, favour the methods by which unemployment figures are calculated. This should not prove too damaging politically; Sir Keith Joseph has argued the need for a reassessment for years.

The question of labour accounting is a minor point, although if it discourages either political party from overreacting to unemployment figures, and guaranteeing higher long-term unemployment by immediately stimulating demand, it will be useful enough. More important is the question of fairness, which to his lasting honour obsessed Mr Heath during the framing of his counter-inflation policy. People will be afraid that re-establishing free collective bargaining will mean that the weakest will go to the wall, not only in money terms but in jobs as well. The socialist economist, Wilfred Beckerman, has made the point in the *New Statesman*:

In the early days of modern capitalism employees could be exploited because their bargaining position was so much weaker than that of their employers. The growth of trade unions, therefore, played a necessary part in rectifying this inbalance, and reducing injustice. But if trade union strength is now to be the instrument through which the stronger and more ruthless unions can exploit their exceptional bargaining power, a new form of social injustice is created. This takes the form of the arbitrary income redistribution that accompanies inflation, and unemployment for many workers in so far as unemployment is the only weapon left to the Government with which to attempt to slow down inflation.

Mr Beckerman's solution is to overhaul wage bargaining machinery, which most unions would take to as kindly as to immediate reinstatement of the Industrial Relations Act. Nor is he right in saying that unemployment is the only weapon left to the Government. It is an ineffective weapon as well as a demoralising one; in our highly benefited, poorly trained and very immobile workforce it is possible for high levels of unemployment to coincide with many thousands of vacancies. What a Government can do, and what a Conservative Government should do, is allow free collective bargaining but *offset the effects through cuts in its own expenditure.* There can be cuts in grants to local government (demunicipalisation of housing); to medicine (compensating the loss by extending tax incentives to employer and employee insurance schemes); to additional expenditure programmes, however dear to ministers' hearts they might be. Cause and effect could likewise be demonstrated by relaxation of price control. Such a 'withdrawal of government' could only, of course, be accomplished *after* the imposition of valorised negative income tax facilities so as to protect the low-paid and elderly. A similar correlation of benefits and allowances within the income tax system would be needed to protect families with children. In other words, means testing without the aggravation.

A programme of this nature is radical, and would take more than one Parliament to accomplish. But it does have great political attractions. Labour ministers, if not the Party, recognise it as the only alternative to wage control and would therefore find some political difficulties in opposing it. It is in line with the Conservative philosophy of greater freedom of choice and greater self-reliance. It is acceptable to shop-stewards, since it stimulates shopfloor choices by contrasting benefits with cash. It coincides with strong public sentiments, again widely held by workers, that the present welfare system attracts those who are capable of working rather than the temporarily deprived or the needy. It might redress the balance, if only a little, between the State and the family.

Another possibility is an appeal to voters', and in particular to unionised voters', common-sense knowledge of the way industry works. (If this sounds patronising, we should remember that only a minority of members of the House of Commons, taking both sides, has working experience of industry.) Out of a workforce of 24 million, about 6 million work in small businesses. Clerical activity absorbs a further 7½ million; the remainder, unionised or not, work in industry. The political difficulties of selling wage restraint without price controls are well known. It should not be difficult to demonstrate, over the heads of union politics and union bureaucracy, that a price ceiling that squeezes profits in relation to wages is from the point of view of any given business or industry equivalent to (and possibly a substitute for) an increase in real wages, or an increase in taxation, or both. Perhaps this will be the greatest service which the Conservative Party and a Conservative Government offer the country: an education in the necessity of viable industrial and commercial activity before the nation of shopkeepers shuts the shop.

Herein lies the importance of industrial democracy. A market approach to our economy, which is increasingly seen by *social democrats* to be the only alternative to full collectivisation, permanent price and income controls, restriction of imports and the like, is all very well as an approach to the arithmetic of things. Its advocates, particularly Tory advocates, whom opponents unjustly present to the public as hard men, need to attend to the essential human element. This is not just a matter of presentation, or public relations; although a society held together by telecommunications demands good public relations. Together with decent wages it may compensate for the uncomfortable truth that modern industrial economies require high output and high-efficiency industries, and that these not only reduce the overall labour requirement but substitute twentieth-century monotony and alienation for nineteenth-century squalor and solidarity. It is of course for industry itself, and for the great trade unions, to discover the forms which the new industrial culture should take. (My own preference is for staggered working, as it liberates the individual for family life.) It is a matter of common sense, not fence-sitting, that the Conservative Party, associated with the boss class in worker imaginations, should take an investigatory rather than an evangelical stance. As Mr John Boyd, General Secretary of AUEW, wrote in a recent issue of *Industrial Society*:

> No government can afford to pass legislation on industrial democracy which workers would be unenthusiastic about . . . The British working class is too mature, too sophisticated, too shrewd and pragmatic to have any sham or hypocrisy about industrial democracy. If any change is coming it must be real. And this throws up the challenge to the trade unions. If indeed we have a whole series of more involvement of workers and their trade unions in management and board level decision-making, will this lead to a divorce of worker representation from workers themselves? This could be a danger.

Here Mr Boyd has put his finger on a central dilemma of the trade unions. Are they to remain worker representatives, competing for a slice of the national pie at the expense of other groups of workers and exercising great but essentially negative power? Or are they to become increasingly involved in the management of a modern industrialised economy and its attendant political system? The worker co-operatives beloved of Mr Benn (and increasingly, it seems, of anti-Keynesian economists like Mr Peter Jay) are unlikely to find the very narrow managerial choices offered by a high-import economy like ours more palatable than leftist leaders find participation in the mixed economy. Nevertheless, there is no need for the Tories to object to workers owning or part-owning their industries, *if* the market is allowed to have some effect on the decisions they make. (In the long term, of course, the market decides whether ventures continue; remember Triumph-Meriden and the *Scottish Daily News*.) Worker shares, or worker representation on boards, are very different matters from State control. As a House of Commons witticism has it: much contemporary nationalisation policy is not robbing the rich to pay the poor so much as robbing the poor to pay the Sheriff.

Conservative philosophy on participation, therefore, must follow that of any open society: allowing and encouraging rational development of an historical process; guaranteeing, in James Prior's words, 'a period of calm in which matters can be worked out through bargaining committees and consultative procedures on the ground'. A mistake made during the 1970–1 period, when the Industrial Relations Act was being framed, was that no concessions on the principles of the Act were to be allowed – so the union leadership boycotted consultations on detail. It is not the business of a Conservative Government to dictate procedures to those directly involved in negotiating a transfer from the negative power of resistance to the positive power of decision. It is, however, the business of the Party as a political organisation to encourage trade unionists to take part in their own affairs and to give special help to Conservative members of unions in putting the Conservative case.

The heart of this case is the survival of the mixed economy in Britain: its capacity to grow and therefore to provide us with the benefits a humane society demands. It is essential that Conservatives learn to persuade the public that there is a connection between levels of manufacturing output and levels of social spending, and to adjust taxation and other policies accordingly. British refusal to pay for the benefits imposed by its political and social system has landed us with debts of such size that we are in danger of borrowing to pay interest on our loans, thereby placing the good fortune of North Sea oil at risk.

It will be said that adjusting taxes to accommodate a truer interpretation of the relationship between productivity and social spending is pinching a leaf from Mr Healey's spring budget of 1976, when he correlated the wage increases permissible under the second phase of his counter-inflation policy with the sums he was prepared to hand out or claw back through control of taxation. So indeed it is; but Conservatives need not in principle object to a Chancellor rendering unto the Exchequer the things that are the Exchequer's, and to the TUC the things that are the

TUC's. There are also crucial differences between the Healey—TUC bargain and the overall adjustment in social spending as well as taxation which we are advocating. The former deceives the unions into thinking that collective bargaining is the governing factor in inflation. The latter involves the whole working population in the facts of working life. High wage claims *combined* with high government spending, with low productivity and overmanning, with inadmissible agreements and demarcation disputes — these are the deadly ingredients of our national decline.

In the decade from 1966 Britain has moved from a cheap food/low wage economy to a dear food/high wage economy. The effects have been traumatic; we should have done it more slowly and we should have done it twenty years ago. Government provision of welfare benefits has failed to adjust to the new situation and the value of money has deteriorated in consequence. This more than anything explains worker uncertainty and unrest and a clear correction will earn a much more positive response. High worker and high managerial rewards are needed in key sectors; central and local government must go without for a time. But as I argued at the beginning, time is in short supply. The vulnerability of our currency places our membership of the Western democracies in danger. Our business is not with palliatives, therefore, but with the choice and chance of renewal.

Index

Index